LARRY SWARTZ

Classroom Events
through
Poetry

D1173328

Pembroke Publishers Limited

For Dad, in memory
For Mom, with love

©1993 Pembroke Publishers, 538 Hood Road, Markham, Ontario L3R 3K9

CREDITS

"After English Class" from *Hey World, Here I Am!* Text copyright © 1986 by Jean Little. Used by permission of Kids Can Press Ltd., Toronto, Canada. Available in the United States from HarperCollins and in the United Kingdom from Oxford University Press. "Cloud Comes" by Jenny Nelson from *Island Rhymes* by Jenny Nelson. Reprinted by permission of the author. "Give Me Books, Give Me Wings." Reprinted with permission of Margaret K. McElderry Books, an imprint of Macmillan Publishing Company, from *I Never Told and Other Poems* by Myra Cohn Livingston. Copyright © 1992 by Myra Cohn Livingston. "I, Says the Poem" by Eve Merriam from *A Sky Full of Poems* by Eve Merriam. All rights reserved. Reprinted by permission of Marian Reiner for the author (1964, 1970, 1973). "The Minute Book" by Julie O'Callaghan from *Taking My Pen for a Walk* by Julie O'Callaghan. Reprinted by permission of Orchard Books (1988). "Out Loud" by Anne Smythe. Reprinted by permission of the author. "The Pen" by Muhammed al-Ghuzzi from *Modern Arabic Poetry: An Anthology* compiled by Salma Khadra Jayyusi. Reprinted by permission from Columbia University Press 1992. "Poems" by Bobbi Katz from *Inner Chimes: Poems on Poetry* compiled by B.S. Goldstein. Reprinted by permission from Boyd's Mill Press (1992). "Poems Can Give You" by Sandra Bogart. Copyright © 1980 Scholastic Canada Ltd., 123 Newkirk Road, Richmond Hill, Ontario, L4C 3G5. All rights reserved. Reprinted by permission. "Sound of Water by Mary O'Neill. From *What Is That Sound!* by Mary O'Neill. Copyright © 1966 Mary O'Neill. Reprinted by permission of Marian Reiner. "Stopping by Woods on a Snowy Evening" by Robert Frost. From *The Poetry of Robert Frost* edited by Edward Connery Lathem. Copyright © 1951 by Robert Frost. Copyright 1923, © 1969 by Henry Holt and Company, Inc. Reprinted by permission of Henry Holt and Company, Inc. "Things" by Eloise Greenfield from *Honey, I Love* by Eloise Greenfield. Reprinted by permission of Harper & Row Junior Books (1978). "Youth" by Langston Hughes. From *The Dream Keeper and Other Poems* by Langston Hughes. Copyright 1932 by Alfred A. Knopf, Inc. and renewed 1960 by Langston Hughes. Reprinted by permission of the publisher. "When It is Snowing" by Siv Cedering from *Color Poems* © 1978. Reprinted by permission of Calliopea Press. "Who Am I?" by Felice Holman from *At the Top of my Voice* by Felice Holman. Charles Scribner's Sons © 1970. Permission of Felice Holman, copyright owner. Care has been taken to trace ownership of copyright material. The publishers will be pleased to receive information that will allow them to correct errors or omissions in subsequent editions.

Canadian Cataloguing in Publication Data

Swartz, Larry
  Classroom events through poetry

ISBN 1-55138-008-0

1. Poetry – Study and teaching (Elementary).
II. Title.

LB1575.S83 1993   372.13'32   C93-094728-2

Editor: Joanne Close   Photography: Ajay Photographics
Design: John Zehethofer   Typesetting: Jay Tee Graphics Ltd.

This book was produced with the generous assistance of the government of Ontario through the Ministry of Culture and Communications.

Printed and bound in Canada by Webcom
9 8 7 6 5 4 3

Contents

Acknowledgements

I would like to give much thanks to those who have helped me shape my poetry teaching and hence, this book:
- all the young poets in Room 203
- all the teachers, in workshops and courses, who listened as I read aloud a poem or two
- The staff of The Children's Book Store, for all their book help.
- Joanne Close, for her pruning and fine tuning
- Sue Checkeris, Brian Crawford and Jim Giles, for their professional support and friendship
- Lois Roy, who was beside me while these poems were being taught
- Finney Cherian, for tomorrow's poems
- Priscilla Galloway, who saw the beginning of this book
- Gordon Wells, who helped me inspect the learning
- Bob Barton, who taught me how to mine poems
- David Booth, who helped me look inside, outside and all around a poem

Preface

I began the first day of school with my grade five class by reciting the poem, "Who Am I?" by Felice Holman.

Who Am I?

The trees ask me,
And the sky,
And the sea asks me
Who am I?

The grass asks me,
And the sand,
And the rocks ask me
Who I am.

The wind tells me,
At nightfall,
And the rain tells me
Someone small.

Someone small
Someone small
But a piece
of
it
all.
Felice Holman

I read this poem to signify the beginning of our journey of learning and experiencing poetry together. *Who Am I?* was appropriate for several reasons — it contains a message of curiosity and reflects my belief that the classroom is a matter of the whole being the sum of its parts.

By year's end, the class had met over three hundred poems — some sad, some funny, some profound, and some silly. Children read works by professional poets and their peers. They wrote and revised their own poems. They read by themselves, in small groups, and as a whole class, always keeping in mind

7

that experimentation with reading, writing, and speaking is key to understanding. Finally, children came to understand what poetry means to many people — solace, joy, pleasure — and what it can mean for them.

It is ironic that one who shunned poetry throughout his school years, who disliked memorization, and who never recited anything beyond couplets has become a promoter of poetry in the classroom. When I was in school, no one told me that poetry could be fun, that I could play with poems, and that I could experience poems in many ways.

This book describes many of the poetry events I shared with my grades three and five classes. These activities can be done in any class with a minimum of preparation and can be modified to suit varying interests and age levels.

The past two decades have been witness to great strides in the area of children's poetry. By not beginning with formal study (formal dissection) of poetry, we now see the value of poetry as an art experience and how using poetry can enhance learning, not only for reading and writing, but also for chanting, singing, discussing, arguing, responding, interpreting, questioning, performing, role playing, painting, and dancing.

Poetry came late to me. As educators, we can ensure that it doesn't come late to today's generation by allowing children to explore and experience the scope of poetry in all its forms.

I

Where Are the Poems?

"I," Says the Poem

"I," says the poem matter-of-factly,
"I am a cloud,
I am a tree.

I am a city,
I am the sea,

I am a golden
Mystery."

But, adds the poem silently,
I cannot speak until you come.
Reader, come, come with me.

Eve Merriam

Creating a Poetry Environment

There are a number of activities that help to establish a poetry environment. These activities, some of which are outlined in this section, require little classroom preparation time — children are immersed in the activity and help to shape its outcome by their reactions to and experiences with the poems.

EVENT 1

Poem of the Day

The "poem of the day" became a ritual in my classroom — a day did not go by that we didn't meet at least one poem. Children liked the idea of encountering a poem each day. On most days, the activity lasted for a few moments while on other days it was incorporated into a response activity that lasted a while or continued throughout the month.

You can begin the event by discussing with the children your goal to feature a poem each day in order to expose them to a variety of forms, a range of poets, and a banquet of words. This can be done by transcribing a poem on a piece of chart paper, which will be displayed at the front of the class. Each morning the class can experience a poem that might be chosen from:

- an anthology,
- a theme,
- a single poet's collection,
- recommendations by others in the school,
- poems children have brought to school.

In addition to reading poems from chart paper, they can be read from overhead transparencies, big books, posters, photo-copied brand-name sheets, or literature anthologies. Children can also bring in poetry anthologies from school, local, and personal libraries. Once the poem has been read aloud, list its title on a chart or calendar posted at the front of the room so that the class has a record of all poems you have experienced together.

S/D	M/L	T/M	W/M	T/J	F/V	S/S
September	November					1
2	3 "This Land Is Your Land" Woody Guthrie	4 "Street Song" Myra Cohn Livingston	5 "Munch Lunch" Arnold Adoff	6 "Hamster...But" Aileen Fisher	7 "Weather Is Full of the Nicest Sounds" Aileen Fisher	8
9	10 "Thanksgiving"	11 "Recipe for Thanksgiving Soup" Dorothy Fornillo	12 "Butterfly" Wendy Cochran	13 "There Came A Day" Ted Hughes	14 "Trees" Harry Behn	15
16	17 "Trip To Book Store"	18 "Hush Little Baby"	19 "Tiny Eeny (Lilian Moore) The Gentle Giant" the Dennis Lee	20 "Owl Questions" David Booth	21 "Goodbye (Geese) Leisure book" Nancy White Carlstrom	22
23	24 "Poems from Halloween Eve meigs"	25 "The Witch "Nightmares" Jack Prelutsky	26 "Dance of the Thirteen Skeletons" Jack Prelutsky	27 "I Met A Dragon" Jack Prelutsky	28 "Ghost of the House Mournes" sean o'huigin	29
	30 31					

✱ Poem of the Week
❀ Poem of the month

OCTOBER

OCTOBRE

10

Children's responses will be as varied as the poem class — closing their eyes, joining in chorally, clapping rhythm, repeating the poem in different voices, raising que: highlighting a word or phrase to savor.

Archibald MacLeish tells us that "a poem should not mean/but be." The "poem of the day" activity honors MacLeish's belief: the few moments that it takes to pour a poem into a classroom demonstrates that poetry matters. By experiencing poems in many ways, children come to discover those they like and, just as important, those that might have remained hidden.

EVENT 2
· · · · · · · · · · · ·
Children's Choices

This activity was a good opener for the first day of school and set the tone for future classroom poetry experiences.

To show that poetry is going to play a significant part of the program, children can be greeted with as many poetry anthologies as you can gather from the school library and personal collections. In my class, I shared the poem, "Who Am I?" before asking each child to select an anthology for the year's first independent silent reading session. The children should be advised that they aren't going to "do" anything with the poems. Rather, the point is to discover the kinds of poems they like. They can be invited to discover what the poems in each of the anthologies might have in common, and perhaps consider what their favorite poem might be as they read through the collection or they could consider a poem they don't understand at first.

The children can select one poem that "spoke" to them and copy it on a large sheet of paper. When the activity is complete, you will have a number of poems that are the children's favorites. Here are the choices my grade five class made, listed alphabetically by poet and accompanied by the anthology in which the poem is found.

Arnold Adoff: "Chocolate Dreams" *Chocolate Dreams*
Anonymous: "The Horny-Galooch" *Amazing Monsters*
A. Nonny Mouse: "A peanut sat on a railroad track" *Poems from A. Nonny Mouse*

11

William Blake: "The Lamb" *Voices on the Wind*
Michael Dennis Brown: "Song for Joey" *Oh, That's Ridiculous!*
Anne Corkett: "This I Know" *Til all the stars have fallen*
James A. Emanuel: "A Small Discovery" *Tomie de Paola's Book of Poetry*
Rose Fyleman: "Mice" *Sing a Song of Popcorn*
Mother Goose: "As I was going out one day" *Tomie de Paola's Nursery Rhymes*
Eloise Greenfield: "Honey, I Love" *Honey, I Love*
Phyllis Halloran: "Enough!" *Red*
Phyllis Halloran: "The Bee" *I'd Like to Hear a Flower Grow*
Langston Hughes: "In Time of Silver Rain" *Snow Towards Evening*
Dennis Lee: "The Garbage Man" *Jelly Belly*
David McCord: "This Is My Rock" *Talking Like the Rain*
Colin McNaughton: "The Vaseline Cheer" *There's an Awful Lot of Weirdos in my Neighbourhood*
Eve Merriam: "Snow in the East" *You Be Good and I'll Be Night*
Jack Prelutsky: "Grasshopper Gumbo" *Something Big Has Been Here*
Jack Prelutsky: "The Troll" *The Headless Horseman Rides Tonight*
Jack Prelutsky: "When Tillie Ate the Chili" *The New Kid on the Block*
Michael Rosen: "I'm just going out for a moment" *Wouldn't you like to know?*
Christina Rossetti: "Hurt No Living Thing" *Animals Animals*
Shel Silverstein: "Ations" *Where the Sidewalk Ends*
Shel Silverstein: "If You Are a Dreamer" *A Light in the Attic*
Judith Viorst: "Night Fun" *If I Were in Charge of the World*
Jane Yolen: "The Cardinal" *Bird Watch*

Each day, one child can share his or her poem with the class. Because children know when their turn is coming, they have a chance to practise playing with voices to capture the poem's mood. Sometimes, children will give an opinion of the poem and discuss why they made their choice or what the poem made them think about.

EVENT 3
. . . .

Poem of the Week

This event provided a nice summary of the ''poem of the day'' activity. Although it took little time, it provided children with the opportunity to reflect on the poems they'd met during the week.

On Friday afternoons, poems can be re-visited and the week's favorite chosen by a quick vote of hands. A star can be placed beside the week's ''winner'' on your class record. ''Education'' by Eloise Greenfield, ''Farmer, Farmer'' by J. Patrick Lewis, and ''I Swim an Ocean in My Sleep'' by Norma Farber were some of the weekly winners in my class.

At the end of each month, the class can also choose the month's favorite poem; at the end of December, March, and June, the term's favorite. Among monthly winners in Room 203 were: ''I'm a Yellow Bill Duck'' by Jack Prelutsky, ''Give Me Books, Give Me Wings'' by Myra Cohn Livingston, and ''Hurt No Living Thing'' by Christina Rossetti.

EVENT 4
. . . .

Poet of the Week

This activity was well-suited to the second half of the year. Children felt comfortable with poems and had begun to identify their preferences in terms of individual poems and poets' styles.

In the second term, the "poem of the day" activity can be modified by featuring a "poet of the week." In Event 39 (pp. 111) we celebrated the work of Eloise Greenfield. Children can work in pairs to search anthologies for works by a single poet, transcribing five of his or her poems that the rest of the class will meet over the course of the week. In addition to choosing poems, children have the opportunity to explore the work of favorite poets. This list represents poets my grade five class chose to highlight.

Jan. 7-11   Dennis Lee
Jan. 14-18   Jack Prelutsky

Jan. 21-25	Eloise Greenfield
Jan. 28-Feb. 1	Arnold Adoff
Feb. 4-8	Roger McGough
Feb. 11-15	Michael Rosen
Feb. 18-22	Shel Silverstein
Feb. 25-29	Myra Cohn Livingston
Mar. 3-7	Jean Little
Mar. 10-14	sean o'huigin

EVENT 5
. . . .

Poetry Selection

This activity promoted a beneficial learning atmosphere for several reasons: it introduced children to a range of poems and anthologies, motivating some children to read poetry independently; children interacted and negotiated with one another, developing the ability to work in collaborative situations; and children began to think critically, moving beyond literal and inferential stages of comprehension.

Monday
Anthologies can be randomly distributed to each child in the class, all of whom have been appointed "judges" of a poetry contest. To begin, the class can brainstorm and discuss criteria to judge their poems.

Each child can choose a "favorite" poem from his or her anthology, using one or more of the criteria written on the chart. Children then copy the poem on a piece of paper.

Tuesday
Children can work in pairs, sharing the poems they chose on Monday. As a pair, they decide which poem they prefer. Each pair of children then matches up with another pair, reads their poems and chooses a favorite. The class will now have between five and seven favorite poems to share. One week's finalists in my class were:

Group 1: "Keepsake" by Eloise Greenfield
Group 2: "Keep a Poem in Your Pocket" by Beatrice Schenk de
 Regniers
Group 3: "Trees" by Harry Behn

Group 4: "If You Are a Dreamer" by Shel Silverstein
Group 5: "Chocolate Dreams" by Arnold Adoff
Group 6: "My Uncle Ronnie" by Michael Rosen.

Wednesday

This is a good time to share a poem with the children that is not among the week's favorite to stimulate discussion. One week, I shared the poem, "The Hunter I Might Have Been" by George Mendoza with the children. The class talked about what the poem reminded them of, how Mendoza conveyed a feeling, and expressed opinions on guns and hunting. Many children raised questions about the poet's intent (e.g., is the poem autobiographical? do you think you could hunt?). Discussing vocabulary, theme, and style in such situations gives children a model for small-group discussions of poems.

Children often returned to "The Hunter I Might Have Been" when stories of war and violence were introduced. One child said that this poet should have read Christina Rossetti's "Hurt No Living Thing" and he might not have shot the bird. We re-read the poem when we read Cynthia De Felice's novel, *Weasel* to discuss the place of hunting in today's society.

Thursday

Children can meet in groups of four to read each of the poems and rank them from most to least favorite, keeping in mind the criteria discussed on Monday. At a class meeting, results can be recorded on a graph.

Friday

Poems can be read to the class. Each child marks a ballot and, after a quick tally, the "winner" can be declared.

One of my students suggested as an alternative activity canvassing teachers in the school, in another class, or their families to determine their favorite poems.

15

EVENT 6
. . . .

Building a Class Anthology

As in Event 5, children had an opportunity to work in a variety of structures while further defining their taste in poetry.

Classroom anthologies can be built around a theme, a topic, or a poetic form. Each child can choose three or four poems from a favorite published anthology. Choices can be narrowed after discussions in pairs, in groups of four, and in groups of eight.

Each child can copy and illustrate a poem. Once the anthology is complete, children might want to give an original title for the collection or borrow a single line from one of the poems. Poems can be bound and copies of the book can be given to another teacher, the school library, and each child in the class.

Building such an anthology respects a child's personal choice and helps him or her to understand choices that professional editors make in creating an anthology. In the classroom, children can act as editors by working as a committee to publish an anthology. At the end of the school year, the class can compile an anthology of poems for the teacher who will be instructing that grade next year.

. . . .

Gathering Poetry Here and There

Over the years, I had acquired copies of books by popular poets such as Shel Silverstein, Jack Prelutsky, and Dennis Lee. I also had some nursery rhyme collections, some anthologies for a humor unit and, of course, a few "black-and-orange" poetry books that emerged each October. Deciding that it was crucial to offer my students an environment rich in poetry, I undertook the task of expanding my collection. Today, I have more than 100 anthologies that have helped, as Georgia Heard (1989) aptly puts it, "marinate" the children in poetry. Unfortunately, because of shrinking school budgets, it is no longer easy to obtain all the resources necessary for a sound program; however, careful buying can still result in an environment rich in literature.

Another source of help can come from parents' associations. As an example, with the support of the school principal, the parents' association at Queenston Drive Public School committed

16

themselves to offering money for each teacher in the school to add books to his or her class library. In the fall, my class visited The Children's Bookstore in Toronto. When the morning was over, each child had selected a new poetry anthology to enrich the class library.

There are many fine anthologies available today for offering poetry to children. To those interested in expanding their poetry repertoire, I recommend that you begin by choosing a book where poems have been collected by theme (*Animals, Animals* by Eric Carle, *Weather Report* by Jane Yolen), by poet (*Hey World, Here I Am!* by Jean Little, *In for Winter, Out for Spring* by Arnold Adoff), or by illustrator (*The Random House Book of Poetry* by Arnold Lobel, *Tomie de Paola's Book of Poems*). (See page 118 for a complete list of recommended books.)

Those using an anthology should become aware of the poet or poems represented, types of poems included, reason for the collection, layout of the poems, use of illustration, and arrangement of poems.

Twenty-five Ways to Collect Poetry

The following list might help you reflect on ways of building a collection that brings poems to children and children to poems.

- ☐ Do you own a favorite poetry anthology?
- ☐ Which anthologies do your colleagues own?
- ☐ Which poetry anthology(ies) can you borrow from the school or community library?
- ☐ How many children have a poetry collection at home?
- ☐ Which poet would you like to celebrate in the classroom?
- ☐ Is there a theme that you would like to make a focus for poetry study?
- ☐ Are there picture books available that might be considered poems?
- ☐ Are there big books available in the primary grades for you to use?
- ☐ Which "readers" are available in your school that feature poetry?
- ☐ Is there a music book in the school that might contain poetry?
- ☐ Which popular song lyrics do you think could be examined as poetry?

17

- ☐ Are there posters available that feature a poem or snippet of a poem?
- ☐ Has part of your classroom budget been directed to buying poetry?
- ☐ Which single poetry anthology would you like to buy from a local bookstore?
- ☐ Are poetry anthologies listed in a book-club brochure?
- ☐ Is there a poet that you could invite to the school?
- ☐ Which verses might you write as an autograph?
- ☐ Are greeting cards available that might feature a poem?
- ☐ Are poems found in a familiar novel?
- ☐ Which poems have the children written that they might share with others?
- ☐ Have you written poems that you might share with the children?
- ☐ What poems are the children's parents familiar with?
- ☐ What are the poems you remember from your school days?
- ☐ What poems do you have in your head?
- ☐ Which poems do the children have in their heads?

II

Poems Out Loud

One Day I Went Walking

One day I went walking
And found myself talking
Out loud!

One day I went running
And found myself humming
Out loud!

Today I went swinging
And found myself singing
Out loud!

Then I heard an echo
From a friendly crowd
Then we all read together
Out loud! Out loud!

Anne Smythe

Teacher As Reader

Like a song, poetry is meant to be experienced out loud. Donald Graves (1992) advises that sharing the sound and sense of a poem can be one of the most delightful moments in the teaching day. When teachers read aloud to children, they become models of reading behavior in phrasing, rhythm, and nuance, thus demonstrating how print holds a richness of meaning. As children listen to their teacher, they create personal images in their minds that can be shared through discussion, writing, art, or drama.

One measure of understanding a poem comes from the way

the poem is recited. Gregory Denman (1988) tells us that working with a poem until it can flow from your tongue with meaning and understanding is the true test of how well you read it. Reciting a poem requires more than memorizing the sequence of words. The poet's intent must be internalized so that the reader becomes familiar with the flavor of the words, their cadence, and flow. Gesture, movement, and involvement illuminate the meaning of a poem. Sometimes it's important to try and identify with the speaker of the poem. Often a change in voice or pace alters the poem's mood and intent. For most children, the poems of their lives come from their teachers' voices; the experience must be a special one to enrich their enjoyment and accelerate their understanding of the poet's art.

The following tips can serve as a guide for reading poems aloud.

• Be prepared to *read aloud occasionally a few poems* by the same poet, or poems on the same topic during one sitting. Children can decide how the poems might connect and identify poems they prefer.

• It is important to *practise privately the reading* of the poem to discover potential trouble spots before you read it to the class.

• Typically, *the whole poem can be read aloud* to the class. Once you begin to read, don't point out a word or ask a question about the meaning of a line. These responses should be left to a time when children can respond to the poem.

• Don't be afraid to *re-read a poem* that children have enjoyed or that has left them confused. On a second or third reading, experiment with voice or pace to alter the way the children listen to and attempt to understand the poem.

• The experience can be made more meaningful by *setting an effective atmosphere*, for example, reading from a special chair.

• At times, *a short discussion* about the poet, title, or theme of the poem can prepare the children for listening. An open-ended question may invite them to contemplate the poem's meaning.

• After reading a poem aloud to the class, *children can read the poem to you*. They might experiment with choral techniques.

• Though it isn't always necessary to *memorize a poem*, it's fun for children to listen to poems or excerpts of poems that you've memorized. Sharing such a piece models your beliefs.

• From time to time, *choose an excerpt* to read aloud. Rather than reading the whole poem, you can read a verse or line to lure the children into listening to the rest of the poem.

Child As Reader

When a child reads aloud, the child's eyes and ears are exploring the rhythms of language. When done well, oral interpretation can improve comprehension skills, helping the child to come to grips with all the meaning to which the words give rise.

Unrehearsed oral reading can be a troubled time for many children. If a child is going to read aloud for an audience, there should be a legitimate reason for doing so and time should be given to practise so that the child can think about what she or he is reading.

In my class, children have read poems aloud on their own in the following contexts.

1. Poem of the Day
Over the year, each child is responsible for reading the poem of the day on four or five occasions. Because the child knows when it is his or her turn, there is an opportunity to work through difficult words or passages and practice their presentation.

2. Sharing Favorites
Often when looking through a poetry anthology, children discover poems they like. When a child says to you, "Hey, look at this neat poem!" the child can read it to you to appreciate its rhythms. Often this is the first time the child has read the poem aloud. It's useful to have the child repeat the reading in order to experience how subsequent readings can change the meaning of the poem. You may also want to re-read the poem with or for the child.

3. Buddy Reading
Our class was partnered with a grade one class in the school. On some occasions we practised reading aloud poems to share with our buddies as they did for us. Also, during independent reading time, many children often buddy up to read poems.

4. Reading Their Own Poems
A child can read aloud poems she or he has written. When the child is ready to share a poem, have him or her read it aloud during a conference so that you can help with the interpretation of the ideas and words.

5. Making a Tape Recording
Making a collective tape recording where each child reads a poem

is another way to practice reading poems effectively. Poems can be chosen according to a theme or can be a celebration of a single poet. Tapes can be left at the listening center or can be shared with parents.

The grade five students had a real opportunity for putting their read aloud skills into further practice in order to create a tape of poems for Bill, a young blind man who worked in our classroom as part of his co-operative education program. When Bill's teaching assignment ended, Janine suggested that the class could prepare a farewell tape of poems for Bill to listen to and enjoy.

Children As Readers (Large Groups)

Bill Moore and David Booth (1988) inform us that when poems are read aloud, the heart and core of the poem emerges. One of the most effective ways to involve children in the enjoyment of poetry is by having them read aloud poems with a partner, with a small group, or as a whole class. When children participate with others within the security of a group, their skill and confidence as readers are boosted.

Children can explore poems by:
- reading in unison;
- repeating lines in response to the leader's call;
- reading one line each;
- reading lines alternately (in two groups);
- reading cumulatively, beginning with a few voices and gradually increasing the number;
- individually reading the lines, with the class joining in on the refrain;
- working in groups on different sections of the poem.

Through shared reading activities (also known as choral speaking, join in, chanting, orchestrated reading), children learn how to manipulate a text. As Bill Martin, Jr. explained to an audience of five thousand teachers at an IRA (International Reading Association) conference, "We do this kind of activity with the children because they are able to transform what they receive and make it their own."

When poems are read aloud, they engage children through the use of repetition, refrain, rhythm, rhyme, and repeated syntactic patterns that may stay with them for life. After hearing many poems, children come to know what different kinds of poetry sound like. Also, by seeing and hearing the selection repeatedly, children come to learn by heart the sight and sound of words.

The following list details other reasons that we need experience strategies where students join together to read aloud.

1. To practice the skills of reading aloud, i.e., pace, pause, pitch, and emphasis
2. To bring to life the words of others by animating print
3. To help readers "hear" what they have read silently
4. To learn by heart the sight and sounds of words
5. To experience the patterns and structures of language (which can be incorporated into their writing)
6. To explore meanings in blocks of print before studying words (i.e., whole poem... verse... line... word... syllable)
7. To boost a child's skill and confidence in the security of a group
8. To experience the rhythm and rhyme, refrain and repetition found in poetry
9. To entertain
10. To recreate in the listener some of the emotions, thoughts, ideas, and dreams of the poet

Poems for Many Voices

Selections for reading aloud should be inherently memorable and draw the children to print. Shared reading is based on the concept that the whole is remembered rather than the part; no attempt at vocabulary and syntactic control is necessary.

Some tips for choosing a read-aloud selection include:
- poems with a definite rhyme scheme;
- poems with a chorus or refrain in which children can join;
- poems in which one or more lines are repeated or echoed;
- question and answer poems;
- poems for two voices (Paul Fleischman's collections, *I Am Phoenix, Joyful Noise*) written in two columns, with some lines read alone and others together;
- poems in which the words imitate or suggest sounds (see "Sound of Water," p. 26);
- list poems;
- poems written in the voice of "apostrophe" (a voice that addresses something that cannot answer);

23

- poems with several verses that can be assigned to groups;
- songs.

Further opportunities for reading poems aloud have emerged from poems of the day, big books, poetry anthologies, and copies of traditional favorites. The following events outline some approaches to choral reading.

EVENT 7
. . . .
Choral Reading (Traditional Couplet)

Because rhyming couplets are brief and rhythmic, they were an ideal way for having children play with their voices, thus helping them to recognize the potential of saying words out loud in many ways.

> Who put the overalls in Mrs. Murphy's Chowder?
> Nobody answered so she said it all the louder

There are a number of activities in which children can take part. This list outlines some suggestions — you may think of others.
- whole class reads lines together
- teacher calls out lines — class responds by echoing teacher
- class is divided into two groups (left/right/front/back, etc.); each group takes a turn to read the couplet
- group 1 calls out first line/group 2 responds (and reverse)
- read repeatedly from loud to soft, from soft to loud
- read repeatedly from slow to fast, from fast to slow
- read with an accompanying clapping rhythm
- group 1 shouts the first line/group 2 whispers the second line (and reverse)
- each word is assigned to different people (solos)
- read as a round with groups starting at different times
- sung (operatic, country and western styles)
- read as if creatures are saying the lines
- read as if someone is frightened
- read as if they're the funniest... saddest... most serious lines ever heard
- read as a secret message
- read as a computer message

24

- broken up — Who put the overalls/in Mrs. Murphy's chowder? Nobody answered/so she said it all the louder!

As an extension, the children can work in pairs to create a rhyming couplet that would be a second verse to the poem. For instance:

She looked in the cupboard the cupboard was bare
She called once again but no one was there

Each pair can decide how to present its couplet by dividing the lines or the words with movement and/or sounds, before presenting the couplet to the group.

Couplets can be compiled on chart paper; children can use the collaborative poem as a source for a class reading.

EVENT 8
· · · · · · · · · · · ·

Choral Reading ("Birthdays")

Sonja Dunn's poems invite oral response — they jump off the page and into the heads (and off the tongues) of her readers. "Birthdays," from her collection, Crackers and Crumbs *was a favorite in Room 203 because children could join in according to their birthdays.*

Birthdays

Hey Hey
When's your birthday

Clap your hands
If it's January

Stamp your feet
If it's February

Shrug your shoulders
If it's March

If it's April
Up you stand

Born in May
Wave your hand

June's the month
To touch the sky

Fly around
If it's July

If it's August
Blow your nose

In September
Touch your toes

If your day is in October
Start that day
By rolling over

In November
Bend your knees

Here's December
You must freeze!

Sonja Dunn

Here are a few activities that encourage experimentation with voice.
- Parts could be assigned according to birthdays.
- Each line could be read alternately; for example, the teacher reads the first line and the class responds by calling out the second line.
- Children can write new lines for this poem by naming new actions to be performed for each month.

EVENT 9
. . . .
Choral Reading (''Sound of Water'')

List poems are a convenient vehicle for choral reading. Single lines can be assigned to various solos. For a ''water'' theme, I asked the children to brainstorm words that represent ''sounds'' of water. After rearranging these words into a list, we read our list poem together. I then shared Mary O'Neill's poem with the class.

Sound of Water

The sound of water is:
Rain,
Lap,
Fold,
Slap,
Gurgle,
Splash,
Churn,
Crash,
Murmur,
Pour,
Ripple,
Roar,
Plunge,
Drip,
Spout,
Skip,
Sprinkle,
Flow,
Ice,
Snow

Mary O'Neill

You can try some of the following suggestions for experiencing "Sound of Water." Children may also have some ideas for reading.
- reading in unison
- read as fast as you can
- read from slow to fast, from fast to slow
- read from loud to soft, from soft to loud
- read at any point, down or up
- read from bottom to top
- group 1 reads from top to bottom/group 2 from bottom to top
- teacher reads the lines; children make sounds that words suggest
- teacher reads one line, group reads alternate lines
- read as a round
- read cumulatively (first child reads the first word, first and second child reading the second word, and so on)

- assign each word to individual members and as a group and ...
  read through the poem as quickly as possible
  read the assigned word in a way that is different from the
    person before
  add a movement as word is read (remain frozen)
  add a sound as word is read (make the sound continu-
    ously until whole poem is finished, then reverse)

As an extension children can choose titles such as "Sound of
School," "Sound of the Playground," "Sound of Winter," or
"Sound of Summer." They can brainstorm sounds they associ-
ate with the title and compile them as a list to create a poem.

Children make decisions about ways to rearrange the words,
for example, by syllables, verbs, or repeating words, and then
read their new poem chorally.

EVENT 10
. . . .
Choral Reading ("What's for Supper?")

*The idea for "What's for Supper?" probably emerged after sharing Jack
Prelutsky's "Bleezer's Ice Cream." I enjoyed playing with various food
combinations and fitting them into a rhyming poem. Poems such as
this one are useful for reading aloud to help the children recognize the
rhyming pattern.*

What's for Supper?

Avocado 'n onion
Mulligatawny stew
Stan's cooking supper
Whatever will we do?

Buttermilk 'n peppermint
Marshmallow 'n beans
Stan's cooking supper
Call for submarines

28

Cauliflower 'n spinach
Artichoke bread
Stan's cooking supper
We're going to be...
grateful!

L.S.

Here are some activities you might like to try with your class.
- children can quickly establish its rhythm and join in to read it aloud and clap
- the teacher can read the lines of the poem, omitting rhyming words (2nd and 4th lines) for the children to call out
- children can write food poems using the pattern of this poem

EVENT 11
. . . .

Choral Reading ("Hints on Pronunciation")

This poem was useful for inspecting how words that are spelled similarly are pronounced differently, thus helping children learn that for most spelling rules there are exceptions.

Hints on Pronunciation

I take it you already know
Of tough and bough and cough and dough?
Others may stumble but not you,
On hiccough, thorough, lough and through?
Well done! And now you wish, perhaps,
To learn of less familiar traps?
Beware of heard, a dreadful word
That looks like beard and sounds like bird,
And dead: it's said like bed, not bead
For goodness sake don't call it "deed!"
Watch out for meat and great and threat
(They rhyme with suite and straight and
debt.)

A moth is not a moth in mother
Nor both in bother; broth in brother;
And here is not a match for there

29

Nor dear and fear for bear and pear,
And then there's dose and rose and lose —
Just look them up — and goose and choose.
And cork and work and card and ward,
And font and front and word and sword,
And do and go and thwart and cart —
Come, come, I've hardly made a start!
A dreadful language? Man alive!
I'd mastered it when I was five.

T.S.W.

The following outline suggests one method for presenting this poem as a class choral reading.
1. Divide lines among children so that some lines are read solo, some as pairs, some by half the class, some by the whole class.
2. Children can experiment with voices to read parts aloud.
3. They read the poem repeatedly and discuss parts that work, identifying those to be changed.
4. Parts that are problematic are reassigned or changed.
5. Children make a choral presentation.

. . . .

Children As Readers (Small Groups)

Small-group choral reading allows children the opportunity to put into practice skills they experienced when reading aloud as a class. More important, small groups enhance children's ability to problem solve in groups — in this instance, how to best present a poem.

Choral reading invites children to use poems as scripts, assigning parts among group members. By working with peers to read aloud poems on a particular theme or by a single poet, they take part in a creative activity that involves variations in voice, sound, gesture, and movement. No two oral interpretations of a single poem are alike because of these variations.

It's interesting to note how each group solves the problem of how to present a poem chorally. If children haven't had much experience reading poems aloud, they usually assign one line to each group member. Given more time, children can experiment with ways of assigning parts, saying words, incorporating movement, and developing effective group formation.

30

The following chart may prove useful in considering ways to introduce choral reading activities to the classroom. Over the course of the year, vary the types of poems, the assignment of poems to groups, and ways the groups are chosen.

Alternative Ways of Introducing Choral Reading Activities		
Choosing Poems	Ways of Working	Groupings
• poems by a single poet • poems on a single theme • poems from an anthology	• each group is given the same poem • each group is given a different poem • a longer poem is divided into parts with each part assigned to a group	• children choose groups • teacher assigns groups • groups chosen randomly (e.g., by counting)

EVENT 12

. . . .

Choral Reading: Presenting a Poem in Small Groups

Children who were familiar with the tune of this traditional rhyme sang the words. By using the poem as a model for choral reading, they experimented with ways of dividing the lines, using their voices and incorporating movement and song.

Hush Little Baby

Hush, little baby, don't say a word.
Poppa's gonna buy you a mocking bird.

If that mocking bird don't sing,
Poppa's gonna buy you a diamond ring.

If that diamond ring turns to brass,
Pappa's gonna buy you a looking-glass.

31

If that looking-glass gets broke,
Poppa's gonna buy you a billy goat.

If that billy goat runs away,
Poppa's gonna buy you a bale of hay.

If you grow up and get real tall.
You'll still be the prettiest baby of all.

Children can form groups of four or five that contain a mix of boys and girls. Each group is given a copy of the poem and asked to read it in a manner of their choice.

Children can read one part alone and one part with one or two others. They can decide which part(s) could be read in unison. The ways children bend these rules make this a creative activity.

Groups might need approximately a half-hour to rehearse their presentations. If too little time is given, children usually are satisfied with a basic interpretation of the poem and might not experiment with choral techniques. Groups shouldn't present unless they feel ready. The negotiating process of deciding how to perform the poem serves the purpose of the activity for some groups.

For this activity, children will work at different paces and levels of commitment and practise, depending on the interaction of group members and their prior experience with similar choral activities. Sometimes, children perform the task smoothly without much intervention. At other times, the teacher will need to negotiate ideas, offering advice in order for them to proceed.

In any class, some groups need more preparatory time than others. When a group thinks that they've ''finished'' while others are struggling to assign parts and experimenting with variations in their presentation, the teacher might serve as a director by identifying a focus the group might consider — finding a new way to stand, assigning different parts to different characters, and so on. Children may not execute a teacher's ideas, but they will recognize the potential for change and polish. In order for the presentation to be successful, children should not be satisfied with an original draft version of their work. Like the writing process, the presenting process requires revising and editing.

Prior to the presentations, the whole class, on a signal, can prepare a final practice. Children will need a few minutes to talk about changes they think are necessary to improve their presentation. Another rehearsal strategy is to have two groups present to each other so that suggestions for improvements can be made. Better yet, the groups could be asked to teach one another their interpretation.

After the presentations, groups can revise parts of their work that were problematic, incorporate audience suggestions, or borrow an idea from another group's presentation.

. . . .

What Is the Learning?

In *Lasting Impressions*, Shelley Harwayne (1993) describes children's work with the traditional poem, "If All the Seas Were One Sea." Each group was responsible for presenting an interpretation of the poem. They were learning to read poems aloud, but there was a richer agenda at stake here — the building of a strong social community in the classroom. Harwayne recognizes that such an activity helps the children to get to know one another, to negotiate, to take turns and to revise, critique, and compliment the work of others. Just as they are asked to revise, clarify, and modify their choral presentations, so will they be asked to revise, clarify and critique their written work and other project work that they present to their peers.

Choral reading is often an enjoyable activity for children since they are able to manipulate a text and be creative about the way they present work to an audience.

Though the activity serves as a context for practising read-aloud skills and presentation is one of the goals, it also serves a more significant function — practising group skills by problem solving. The nature of the task demands that each group member offer ideas or challenge the ideas of others. Everyone is responsible for making contributions and decisions about the group's final presentation; children are practising group skills that will, at any time, comprise argument, challenge, negotiation, compromise, criticism, and encouragement.

In order for children to understand the potential of such activities, it's important that they have opportunities to reflect on their learning through talk or written response. They can consider the part they played in the group, as well as the part played by group leaders (if they were not the group leader), how ideas were arrived at, how problems were solved, how they negotiated ideas, what changes were made, and reasons for these changes.

33

The Group and You

- Was there a leader in your group?
- Were you a leader much of the time? sometimes? rarely?
- How did the group receive your ideas and contributions?
- How did you receive the ideas and contributions of others?
- Were you ever frustrated?
- How did you handle ideas that you didn't like?
- Did you co-operate with your group all of the time?
- Were you and your group "on task" all of the time?
- Which idea(s) in the presentation was yours?
- Did anyone tell you what to do, or did you decide on your part yourself?
- Are you satisfied with your presentation?
- What would you change about your presentation?
- Did the teacher influence/interfere with your work?
- What did you enjoy about the activity?

Reflecting on Your Presentation

- Were you familiar with your part(s)?
- Were some parts read as solos, others read together?
- Was your presentation too busy? Could you change some of your ideas so that the presentation is clearer?
- Did everyone have an equal part in the presentation?
- Could your part be heard, even if you read in a whisper?
- Were you aware of an audience, looking at them as often as possible?
- Was there variety in the voices you used?
- Did you stand or sit as you were performing, did you lean on furniture, put your hands in your pockets, and so on?
- Did you distract others as they spoke?
- What was unique about your group's presentation?
- Did you add sound effects to enhance your presentation?
- Was there movement or gesture in your presentation?
- If you had more time to rehearse, what would you change?
- Could you present the poem without looking at a copy?

The more children participate in such activities, the better their work will become. As they work with a number of poems and group formations, their learning will differ. Exposure to choral reading enriches read-aloud, presentation, and group skills.

The questions on the preceding page will help children assess their learning with choral reading presentations. Questions can be answered privately, discussed in small groups, or shared with the whole class.

Time to Present

For presentation at a school concert or assembly one useful strategy is to have the whole class present a single poem chorally and then have small groups present a poem that they have prepared on a particular theme or topic. As an example, for one assembly, the lines of Bill Martin Jr. and John Archambault's "Listen to the Rain" were assigned to various children in the grade three class. Children, in small groups, presented other poems about rain that they had rehearsed ("Listen to the Rain" by Sonja Dunn; "To Walk in Warm Rain" by David McCord; "I Am the Rain" by Grace Nichols; and "April Rain Song" by Langston Hughes).

For the school's winter concert, the class prepared a choral reading of the song, "What a Wonderful World" by Louis Armstrong and the poem, "There was Once a Whole World in the Scarecrow" by Brian Patten. We combined the two so that the weaving of words presented a contradiction of themes and messages about caring for the world. For the assembly, each child read aloud at least one line of the text and a videotape was shown of the children moving to the song. Here is an excerpt:

I see trees of green
    The farmer has dismantled the old scarecrow
Red roses too
    He has pulled out the straw and scattered it
I see them bloom
From me and you
    The wind has blown it away
And I think to myself
    A mouse once lived in its straw heart
What a wonderful world . . .

EVENT 13
· · · · · · · · · · · ·

Presenting a Longer Poem

One of the most appropriate strategies for presentation is to divide a longer poem among groups. A grade four teacher at my school worked with her class to present a choral presentation of Byrd Baylor's piece, I'm in Charge of Celebrations. *The class was divided into five groups; each group presented a section of the poem. The choral work was introduced with dance dramas about celebrations, created by the children. The presentation was also accompanied by frozen tableaux representing the celebrations described in the book.*

When a poem is divided into a number of verses, one or two sections can be assigned to various groups. If there are no distinct verses, the poem can be divided arbitrarily and each group assigned a part to present. In groups, children can make decisions about the best way to present their excerpt.

You can visit the groups as they work to determine if they need assistance or direction. Remind them of the range of options they can draw on — sound effects, props, lighting considerations, movement — to enhance their presentation.

After children have rehearsed, they can present the poem in its entirety with each group presenting its part dramatically.

Such poems as "The Jumblies" by Edward Lear, "Arithmetic" by Carl Sandburg, and "The Cremation of Sam Magee" by Robert Service are useful for this type of choral activity. For older students, Maya Angelou's poem, "On the Pulse of the Morning" would be a rich experience for many voices.

III

How Words Fit

The Pen

Take a pen in your uncertain fingers.
Trust, and be assured
That the whole world is a sky-blue butterfly
And words are the nets to capture it.

Muhammad al-Ghuzzi

Snippetry

In his book, *Words That Taste Good* word scavenger Bill Moore (1987) explores more than 600 short, sharp bits of poetry to stimulate interest in the power of words. He explains, "poets work with words and words are peculiar things. They are very hard to pin down. They slither away from you and yet they are the very best way of conveying ideas, thoughts and emotions" (p.2).

EVENT 14

Collecting "Snippets" of Poetry

In order to have children inspect the way poets fit words together, I asked children to create a classroom display of short bits from poems, as Moore had done for his book. The result was a collection of "snippets" — some sad, some funny, some thought-provoking.

Children can choose two to four lines of poetry that they think convey images. They can write the lines on pieces of cardboard and display them in the classroom for others to contemplate.

By choosing isolated lines from the beginning, middle, or ending of a poem, children have an opportunity to linger over words that they think "taste good." Although they will first pay attention to the meaning of the whole poem, this activity stimulates them to look at bits of language and determine how words arranged in patterns enlighten our imaginations and feelings.

EVENT 15
. . . .
Creating Poetry Graffiti

One afternoon, I noticed that the bulletin board hanging outside our classroom door was hungry for a display so I suggested to the class that we transform it into a graffiti board of poetry "snippets." Children enjoyed creating the board, which enlivened the hall.

Children can be invited to choose two to four lines from a favorite poem, and write them as a piece of graffiti with a poet's name accompanying the message. They can illustrate the poems using materials of their choice. The activity can be theme-based or the children can select their favorite snippets to display.

Poetry invites children to pay attention to words and treat them with respect. Through poetry, teachers can help children to discover how familiar words can surprise us, how new words can possess us. It allows children to experience the shapes, sounds, images, and meanings of words. Rather than define the terms of metaphor, simile, alliteration, and personification, children become aware of how poets use language. When they're ready to discover how the poet accomplished an effect, and the name given to it, teachers can provide information and instruction about literary techniques.

I heard a bird sing
in the dark of December
A magical thing
And sweet to remember.

"Freezing" the Poems We Know

Transcription exercises result in a written record of talk. Children release the rhymes in their head and preserve them in frozen written form. As children put pen to paper, they explore forms of poetry, giving careful consideration to line breaks, white spaces, and verse formations. The activity provides children with a context for listening carefully to the sound of words as they explore rhythms and rhymes, refrain and repetition. The publishing aspect of the activity focuses their attention on spelling, punctuation, and handwriting.

EVENT 16
. . . .
Treasure Hunt

One way to have children look at poems up close and examine how words

39

fit is to have a ''treasure hunt'' to discover how words and lines from various poems fit certain criteria. I began this activity by composing a list of generic questions that children answered by referring to an anthology. An extension to this activity had children working in pairs to make their own list of 10 to 15 items that they traded, along with the anthology they used to form the items, with classmates who tried to complete the list.

Children can work in pairs for this activity. Each pair can be given an anthology, along with a copy of the following activity sheet. A time limit of 45 minutes can be imposed for each pair to complete as many items as possible. Most anthologies will contain examples of each item on the list; however, if a pair is unable to find an answer, they can leave it blank. When the time has expired, children can share their answers in groups of four.

A Treasure Hunt

- Find a line of poetry that mentions an animal.
- Find a line of poetry that mentions a color.
- Find a line of poetry that mentions the name of a person or place.
- Find two lines of poetry that rhyme.
- Find three pairs of rhyming words.
- Find a line of poetry that is four words long.
- Find a line of poetry that has ten syllables.
- Write the title of the last poem in the book.
- Write the first line of the first poem in the book.
- Write the last two lines of the second poem in the book.
- Copy a poem that is less than twenty-five words.
- Write a title that made you smile.
- Identify the most unusual looking poem and identify reasons for your choice.
- Write three questions about your book for others to answer.
- Write the year the book was published.
- Choose an alternate title for the book.
- Find out if there is an index of first lines. Write the title of the first poem in the index.

Recreating Poems

At times, poetry serves as a stimulus for art activities in our program — I often use literature as a source for illustration and believe visual responses to poetry are another way for children to reveal images that have entered their minds as they listened to or read a poem.

The following events describe strategies that provide opportunities for children to recreate poems from words to pictures.

EVENT 17
. . . .

Compiling School Rhymes

A friend who was preparing an anthology of skipping, playground, and street rhymes asked my class to conduct a research project on popular school rhymes for a unit on contemporary "recess rhymes" in the book Doctor Knickerbocker. *The class undertook the task with gusto, and in the process gained valuable experience in listening and speaking, transcribing and presenting material.*

To begin, the class can brainstorm familiar rhymes. In our class, we compiled a list of 125 titles, including: "A sailor went to sea, sea, sea;" "Jingle Bells/Batman smells;" "Eenie Meenie Pepsi Weenie;" "Teddy Bear, Teddy Bear;" and "Miss Mary Mack Mack Mack."

Once the list is complete, several rhymes can be assigned to each child. Children have the opportunity to transcribe and illustrate the rhymes. You can help them with this activity by outlining how their work will be gathered to produce a class book.

During the project, children have the opportunity to chant, clap, and sing familiar rhymes individually, in small groups, and as a whole class. The activity successfully integrates listening and speaking, reading and writing as children work from verbal activities to print, and from print to verbal activities.

41

EVENT 18
. . . .
Songs As Poems

This event began with the work of four students who wanted to transcribe the song, "From a Distance" by Bette Midler. The activity quickly caught on with other groups of children who transcribed a number of songs, including "Imagine" by John Lennon and "What a Wonderful World" by Louis Armstrong. Like the rhyme event, listening and transcribing are integral to this activity.

Children, in small groups, can choose a song and listen carefully to a taped version. They can then transcribe what they think are the words of the song. Once children have decided on the words, they record them on paper and divide the lines in ways they think transform the song to a poem. Time should be made available for groups to revise their work, for example, changing line lengths and correcting spelling and punctuation errors. When groups have finished their revisions, they can trade their "poem" with another group and read the works chorally.

. . . .

Playing with Free Verse

When many teachers think about poetry, they associate it with forms such as rhyme, haiku, cinquain, sonnet, and ballad. For these teachers, instructing children to write in fixed forms is the norm. For a number of other teachers, however, free verse poetry is an attractive alternative, allowing poets to find form in the rhythm and content of what they are saying.

I had the opportunity to attend a presentation by Georgia Heard and was intrigued by the way she helped the audience find an understanding of free verse poetry. Heard, who thinks that an emphasis on fixed form may distort the meaning of writing poetry, explained to the crowd that just as units of organization in prose are the sentence and the paragraph, units of organization in poetry are the line and the stanza. To prove her point, she presented us with the task of transforming several lines of prose into poetry by re-shaping line lengths and white spaces. I enjoyed the activity; the speaker's point about the possibilities of molding poems in many ways was well taken.

42

EVENT 19
· · · · · · · · · · · ·

Experimenting with Free Verse

This event details a similar activity I introduced to my class to help them experience free verse writing. For this activity, I presented the children with the poem, "Minute Book" by Julie O'Callaghan from her collection, Taking My Pen for a Walk.

Minute Book

I will give each hour
a name
so that, when I'm dying
I will look at them again,
point to some and smile
"that hour was my friend."

Julie O'Callaghan

To begin, you can demonstrate how the activity might be done by using two lines from a novel. Concepts of line breaks and white spaces can be discussed with the children by showing examples from different poets. Also, we reviewed poems by Arnold Adoff where some lines contain only one word, others two or more. We inspected how his poems had varying line lengths, and were sometimes written as if scattered on the page.

Instead of writing the poem as Julie O'Callaghan did, you can write the words as prose (i.e., one continuous sentence without line breaks). Children can form groups of four or five to shape the words into a poem by dividing the lines.

This activity fulfils the goal of seeing how words can be arranged freely, sometimes resulting in a poem. It is a healthy talk activity where children can argue, negotiate, question, describe, and explain the way that they think the poem should look. As a co-operative learning activity, it provides everyone with an opportunity to assess how they function in groups.

Indeed, in our class, each group presented the poem differently. One group wrote the poem in the shape of a clock, which remained on display throughout the year beside the real clock, confronting children as they watched the minutes pass.

EVENT 20
· · · · · · · · · · · ·

Creating a Class Mural

If there is one poem that my students have taken to heart it is Christina Rossetti's "Hurt No Living Thing." When our school decided to hold an environment convention, we chose to display the poem as part of our contribution to the event. Using old copies of National Geographic, *children cut out the letters of words in the poem and mounted them on a large mural. The project was a true co-operative venture where each child contributed to the presentation of the poem as billboard in order to attract a wide audience.*

To begin, children can help to create a background by combining large sheets of white mural paper so that you have a rectangle of approximately 3 meters x 4 meters. Divide the words of the poem you are presenting on the mural so that each child is responsible for cutting out letters for two or three words. If possible, supply the children with old magazines that relate to the theme you are studying.

After the letters are cut out, ask the children to form committees whose task will be to arrange and glue the words onto the large mural paper so that the poem fills the whole sheet. The class can decide if other features are needed to enhance the presentation of the poem.

EVENT 21
· · · · · · · · · · · ·

Banners

Throughout Queenston Drive Public School hang beautiful batik banners, each featuring a snippet of poetry. Children in two classes selected the snippets and created the banners with the help of Dorothy Caldwell, a gifted teacher and artist. Funded in part by the Ontario Arts Council, Dorothy spent three weeks helping the children learn the art of batiking. For her project, we decided to use poetry as a focus for the panels. While you may not have the guidance of a batik artist, the activity is feasible with the help of a knowledgeable staff member, or you can create other types of banners using a medium of your choice.

To begin, each child can pick a favorite poem from an anthology and choose two to four lines of poetry that they think are particularly effective. For the first art activity, they can write their snippets on large sheets of chart paper and illustrate them using crayon pastels, poster paints, or other media.

For the next stage, help the children to simplify, enlarge or change their original drawings. (Clear, strong images with simple lines work best.) Children then draw the images in marker on large sheets of newsprint. Over a three-day period, they add wax outlines and color them with ink dyes. Once complete, children can add the words to the poem using fabric markers. When finished, panels can be hung in three to make banners.

EVENT 22
. . . .
Poems As Picture Books

There are several picture books that feature single poems. Listen to the Rain, Annabel Lee, *and* Stopping by Woods on a Snowy Evening *(see pg. 122) are examples where one or two lines are accompanied by*

45

a full-page illustration. Using these books as models, the class can create a picture book based on a favorite poem. In our class, we illustrated "There Was Once a Whole World in the Scarecrow" using colored tissue paper and white glue mixed with water. Pictures were created on white cardboard and the book was assembled for others to read.

You can begin this activity by showing children examples of books that feature a single poem, such as those listed previously. Children can think of poems they know that would make effective picture books. You can record their suggestions and help them make a final selection of the poem they will illustrate.

Depending on the length of the poem, each child can be assigned one or two lines to illustrate. Children can decide as a class how they are going to illustrate the book (e.g., paints, markers, collage). When each child has finished their page, their work can be collected and the pages collated to make a book. The book can be donated to the library or kept in the classroom.

EVENT 23
. . . .

Illustrating Poems

To help children understand the power of illustration, I've often used poetry as a source for art, discussing how pictures help tell a story or depict an image. We have looked at various media that artists have used, including Eric Carle's collage techniques for Animals Animals, *Kadie MacDonald Denton's use of watercolor for* Til All the Stars Have Fallen, *Quentin Blake's humorous black-line drawings for Michael Rosen's poetry collections,* Wouldn't You Like to Know *and* Quick! Let's Get Out of Here, *and Warabé Aska's glorious paintings for* Seasons, Aska's Animals, *and* Aska's Birds.

An effective activity that helped children appreciate the importance of illustration was to ask them to imagine they were illustrators of poetry anthologies.

Unlike the previous event, where students worked collaboratively to illustrate one poem, this event has children working individually. You can begin by discussing with the children the fact that

46

they are illustrators who have been approached by poets to illustrate their works. In order to illustrate the poems, they should consider the message the poet is trying to convey and determine the appropriate type and content of illustrations. My class found water-based markers were effective. Once students have prepared their drawings, they use a brush and water to make the marker lines bleed — the effect is watercolor-like and has a rather "poetic" quality.

Ask the children to pick a poem they would like to illustrate. They can use water-based markers as my class did or they can choose another type of illustration. Poems and illustrations can be displayed in the school or community or assembled into a class anthology.

Brother Sun, Sister Sky

47

IV

Inside the Poem

Poems Can Give You

Poems can give you
double vision.
They make you see
the colours you feel
when you're sad,
the sound of a red,
red sunset,
the smell of happiness,
the flavours of the seasons,
Double vision
not blurred
but crisp as last night's snow.

Sandra Bogart

Making Sense of Poetry

As a teacher of reading, I became interested in discovering what happens in the minds of readers as they actively engage in reading texts. Recognizing the essence of reader response theory, I have come to understand that what the reader brings to a text is part of the construction of the literary experience. The finding of meanings, as Louise Rosenblatt (1938) informs us, involves both the author's text and what the reader brings to it.

Early in the year, I asked a group of children to tell me, in one word, what they thought was the theme of the poem, "There Was Once a Whole World in the Scarecrow" by Brian Patten.

Responses included: *death, life, destruction, moving, pollution, ecosystems, change,* and *inconsideration.* The point, of course, is that none of these readers is wrong. The importance of a work of literature is an individual matter.

The implication for the classroom is that as teachers we should be making every effort to recognize all individual responses, not only because they reveal something about the thinking and culture of the reader, but because we will be helping students to discover the meaning of poetry — and other literary genres — for themselves.

To further demonstrate the importance of personal response, it is worth mentioning a story shared by Nancie Atwell (1991) in the article, "When Readers Respond" that appears in her collection of essays, *Side by Side.* As part of a course that she taught on responding to reading, Atwell describes an experience of forty high school and university English teachers mapping their way through a reading of a poem that none had read before. Atwell explains that there were no two remotely similar accounts of the process of reading the poem. In this instance, expert readers who spent regular time discussing literature had responses that were distinctly personal and idiosyncratic. Through listening to each other's responses, returning to the text, and coming back to talk about it over the next few days, the group agreed about the "meaning" of the text. How in our classrooms can we provide that same type of community for sharing that these literate adults encountered in exploring a poem?

Spontaneous Responses to a Short Poem

The responses to the following ten-word poem by Jenny Nelson offered an opportunity for the children to learn how we each have different thoughts about the texts with which we engage.

I wrote the poem on a piece of chart paper and invited the children in my grade three class to respond spontaneously by recording whatever came to mind after they read the three lines. They used index cards to record their short, immediate thoughts.

> Cloud comes
> Drinks up the sea,
> And spits on me.

When the children completed their responses, they shared their thoughts with others at the table and quickly recognized how their neighbors had similar or different thoughts. I collected their responses and classified them into four categories.

State Opinions
- I like the poem because it's short but it still tells a story and makes you think.
- It's hard to respond to because it's too short.
- The poet tells me about how rain storms happen in an easy way so that we can understand it. I like the poem.

Raise Questions
- I don't understand how the cloud drinks the sea. How did the cloud come in the first place?
- Is there another verse to this poem?
- Where did she get her idea from?

Make Personal Connections
- It makes me think about rain, the sea, taking a shower, drinking water, washing dishes, water balloons, wetting my hair, and falling in a puddle.
- When I finished reading this poem I thought of Niagara Falls.
- It reminds me of yesterday. It rained and I was going camping. I wanted to go roller blading but I couldn't so I stayed in and played Nintendo. When the rain stopped I went to my friend's and then I went roller blading.

Make Analogies
- The story is like a fountain, because it's the same cycle. It goes up the pump (gets evaporated) and then comes out of the tap (the clouds). This poet must like rain or cycles.
- This reminds me of the other rain poem that we did last week. In the other poem the person liked the rain, but I don't know if he would have thought it was spit.
- The cloud is like a person because people drink and clouds really don't.

What do children learn from an activity such as this? For one thing, they recognized that their peers had a range of responses, . some similar to their own, others quite different. Because I

50

accepted all responses, the children came to trust that their opinion mattered regardless of whether they liked the poem or understood it. Also, the children were able to learn about aspects of the poem from one another, rather than the teacher. It was Bobbi who pointed out that there is a rhyme in the poem, Jeffrey who explained how clouds make rain, and Sari who talked about personification when he said the cloud is like a person drinking. The poem also provided an opportunity for them to share memories, whether it was about a trip to Niagara Falls or playing indoors during a windy weekend.

In addition to honoring personal responses, this poem provided an opportunity to discuss some of the stuff of poetry. Through these three lines, we discussed the story the poem told, the way the poet makes the cloud behave as if it were a person, and the use of surprise at the end. The topic of the water cycle led to library investigation in order to gain more information.

Finally, though the poem is a short one, the children's experience with it taught them about the process of making meaning. When they meet longer poems, they will be able to recognize some of the thinking and interpretations that arose with "Cloud Comes." Gregory Denman (1988) explains that interpretation and meanings are not creatures born whole and correct, but emerge from bits and pieces. "What we learn along the way in coming to meaning," Denman points out, "is certainly more valuable than our final view" (p. 85).

A child reads a poem such as "Cloud Comes" to better read another, and in turn, another. Perhaps the child will return to "Cloud Comes" and get something more from it.

Each poem that a child encounters has something to teach him or her about poetry. The more a child learns, the more proficient she or he becomes as thinking, wondering readers/responders. Hopefully, an experience such as this prepares children for other poems they will discover during the year, their school career, or their lives.

Written Responses to a Poem

Early in the year, I chose to introduce Siv Cedering's poem, "When It Is Snowing" to the grade five class because of the visual image that it conveys. I felt it was a compact example of free verse and, since we had already encountered several poems about birds, it would likely provide a range of responses for us to consider.

When It Is Snowing

When it is snowing,
the blue jay
is the only piece of sky
in my
backyard.

Siv Cedering

As I read the poem aloud to the children, I asked them to copy it into their journals. Many children wrote the poem as a complete sentence, not paying attention to the form that Siv Cedering chose to paint her word canvas.

The children responded to the piece by explaining whether they thought this was a poem or not. I invited the children to elaborate on their responses by discussing what the poem reminded them of or how it made them feel.

After the children completed their journal entries, I instructed them to share their responses and discuss their opinion of the poem with others who were seated at their tables.

As I wandered about the room, it was interesting to hear Miranda argue that it was a poem while the rest of her group said it wasn't; to hear James puzzle over why the poet talked about the blue jay as a piece of sky when there are other birds that fly in the sky; and to discover Liza asking questions about when this took place, what else was happening as the blue jay landed in the backyard, and why the poet wrote the poem.

After the small-group discussion, the children were asked to write in their journals to clarify or change their initial response, or to add a new thought or question about the poem.

Finally, we had a whole-class discussion about whether this was a poem or not and worked toward defining a poem.

There are a number of ways children can share their written responses to poems that they meet privately or that are introduced to the whole class. If reading response journals are used in the program, children can record some of their thoughts as they would any other piece of literature. They can also respond on a separate piece of paper or a file card because it invites succinctness.

Most responses will be recorded after the children have read the poem, though in some cases they may respond to a poem's title or record some of their thoughts and questions as they read the poem bit by bit. Written responses can be shared with the teacher or with peers. Further learning can arise when children share what they have written with others and discover what others may have thought. This can be done in small groups or with the whole class.

Sometimes, children may respond in writing after discussing a poem with others. This allows the child to reflect on what has been said and articulate what she or he has taken from the poem or discussion.

The more familiar children become with personal response, the more apt they are to share their thoughts and opinions about a text. Though children are encouraged to respond to a poem in "any way," at times they might need some questions to guide their response.

Ten Questions to Guide a Child's Response

1. Can you say in one sentence what this poem is about?
2. What is it about this poem that you particularly liked? disliked?
3. What did this poem remind you of?
4. What things in this poem did you see? hear? taste?
5. What are some questions or puzzles that you have about this poem?
6. Did this poem give you any special feeling(s)?
7. How did the poet use words or groups of words effectively?
8. How is this poem different from/the same as other poems you have read?
9. What would you tell or ask the poet about the poem?
10. How is this a poem?

The Teacher's Response

Just as I asked the class to share thoughts in their journals, I wrote a two-page response to "When It Is Snowing," thus demonstrating my own reading process to the children.

I tried to think of my backyard where I grew up in downtown Toronto. On a winter's day, I'm sure I would have seen very little color as I looked out my bedroom window. For the poet, the blue jay is the only spash of color, a splash that arouses a feeling in the poet.

It might have been just a quiet image she wrote while sitting at her computer. I see the poet struggling over a piece of writing, then glancing out the window, seeing a blue jay and then taking a polaroid snapshot that develops into sixteen words, thus giving birth to this poem.

Inspecting Children's Responses

Siv Cedering's poem initiated a significant response activity in our classroom. Not only did the "analysis" of the poem help the children realize that there is no single answer to the meaning of the poem, but the analysis of their written comments allowed me to assess their responses through a developmental framework.

Using Jack Thomson's *Developmental Model of Process Stages* (1981), I attempted to assess the students' process stages by fitting their written responses into Thomson's framework. The following chart outlines my analysis.

PROCESS STAGES	RESPONSE JOURNAL ENTRIES	STUDENT
Kinds of Satisfaction		
1. Unreflective Interest in Action	It is a poem because the blue jay is blue and so is the sky.	Alan
	I think that this poem's about nature. So does Janine.	Lisa
	It is short.	Billy
2. Empathizing	This poem makes me feel like the blue jay on the fence looking at the snow on the ground.	Miranda
3. Analogizing	It is a poem because how it is shaped when we done the other poem "The Minute Book."	Jagpal
	We are a little piece of the earth and he is a little piece of the sky.	James C.

54

	This poem makes me think of my cottage. At my cottage, there are lots of birds there. There are blue jays and robins and the chipmunk family that lives under the deck. It made me think of how my grandpa got a blue jay to come and eat peanuts out of my hand.	Heidi
4. Reflecting on significance of events	To me I would think it's a miracle to see nature passing by. Why did the blue jay choose to go to that back yard?	Georgette
Reflecting on significance of events (interrogating text)	What is taking place in the back yard?	Liza
	Some parts I don't understand because other birds can also be a piece of sky.	James
Reflecting on significance of events (theme)	It makes me feel glad about birds. Because birds are the most colorful animals in the world. If we don't have birds, they wouldn't sing for anyone.	Ricky
5. Reviewing whole works as author's creation	I was thinking how she could have changed a paragraph into a poem.	Sunil
	In my mind I picture a blue jay flying across a backyard of white snow with two gates and I picture a little house and someone looking out of the house watching a blue jay with his hand over his cheeks. And I picture a stream behind the gate. We all had different pictures in our heads.	Christi
6. Consciously considered relationship with text	I like this poem it's nice because it is so peaceful. I closed my eyes. I saw white snow.	Shannon

The journal entries helped me recognize the levels children were at in their development as readers. Analysis of these responses through Thomson's framework confirmed a basic assumption that I held about the uniqueness of every reader.

At the end of the activity, Miranda asked if we could do the activity again. Maybe it was the poem that she enjoyed, maybe it was the realization that her response was being validated along with everyone else's in the class. I felt that Miranda was coming to recognize the children's potential as meaning-makers, and hoped that she, with her peers, would apply this to future readings of poems and other texts as they read independently.

"When It is Snowing" appears in an excellent collection by Paul Janeczko (1990) entitled *The Place My Words Are Looking For*, which contains poems and reflections of thirty-nine leading poets. As a bonus to our work, I shared with the class some of Siv Cedering's thoughts about the poem. "Like the blue bird, a poem is often small, but it can surprise you. With words it can paint a picture that in turn leads to other pictures and thoughts. So when you see a poem, read it as carefully as you would open a surprise package. And someday when it is snowing, or some night when everyone is asleep, try writing a little poem" (p. 117).

Putting It Together

When children play with poems by rearranging words, phrases, and lines, they can experience the way the poet has put words together at the same time they interact with the meanings a poem may have created with their experiences.

EVENT 24
. . . .

Jumbled Lines 1

Children who enjoy puzzles and games responded well to this activity. Short, unrhymed, poems are most suitable, usually with a maximum length of fifteen lines. Langston Hughes's "Youth" is a suitable choice for this activity.

56

Youth

We have tomorrow.
Bright before us
Like a flame.

Yesterday
A night-gone thing,
A sun-down name.

And dawn today
Broad arch above the road we came.
We march!

Langston Hughes

Children can be provided with lines of a poem that have been taken out of order. They can work in pairs to organize the lines in their original order. When each pair has reorganized the poem, they can share their version with another pair.

Before you read the original version aloud, you might want to ask the class as a whole to attempt to build up the poem, line by line.

EVENT 25
. . . .
Jumbled Lines 2

This activity allowed the children a lot of flexibility and creativity and served as a good follow-up to the previous event.

Children can work in pairs or on their own for this activity. Write out a poem and cut each line as a separate strip of paper. Children can arrange the lines in the way they think is most suitable. They can also eliminate lines or cut their strips to make more lines in the poem.

When children are satisfied with their final version, they can glue the poem on to a piece of construction paper. In groups, children can compare the ways they presented their poems. As part of this discussion, children can explain their reasons for arranging the poem as they did.

As a final activity, you can read the original version aloud. Children can discuss how the meaning of the poem changes by the way the lines are organized.

V

Talking About Poems

After English Class

I used to like "Stopping by Woods on a Snowy
Evening."
I liked the coming darkness,
The jingle of harness bells, breaking — and adding to
— the stillness,
The gentle drift of snow...

But today the teacher told us what everything stood for.
The woods, the horse, the miles to go, the sleep —
They all have "hidden meanings."

It's grown so complicated now that,
Next time I drive by,
I don't think I'll bother to stop.

Jean Little

The Poetry Club

When I was teaching grade three, a group of former grade five students approached me about forming a book club. When I suggested that they form a poetry club instead, the seven children agreed to try my suggestion. They decided to meet once a week for fifty minutes. During that time, they would discuss and play with poems, some chosen by me, some by them. Group dynamics reflected some classroom procedures to which the children were already accustomed; that is, group members would share their reading of a poem and listen to their peers' reactions, reflections, comments, and questions about what they'd read.

We brainstormed a list of activities that interested club members and drew up the following agenda that provided variety in discussion, writing, drama, and art activities.

The following list outlines the various activities that *The Poetry Club* was involved in.

Meeting 1 — Review classroom anthologies/set an agenda
Meeting 2 — Share favorites/discuss "Stopping by Woods on a Snowy Evening" by Robert Frost
Meeting 3 — Discuss the poem "Famous" by Naomi Shihab Nye (an open agenda without the teacher)
Meeting 4 — Create a graffiti wall of snippets from poetry
Meeting 5 — Choral speaking
Meeting 6 — Drama/Scene One from the play "Skin" by Dennis Foon
Meeting 7 — Poems by Langston Hughes and James Berry
Meeting 8 — A "poetry contest": Which poem would you choose?
Meeting 9 — Brainstorm: What makes a poem good?
Meeting 10 — Discuss (with the teacher) the poem "Lines" by Judith Nicholls
Meeting 11 — Reassemble jumbled lines of a poem
Meeting 12 — Write a poem about reading
Meeting 13 — Buddy with grade three students to revise poems
Meeting 14 — Use the first line of a poem (from Index of first lines) to write a poem
Meeting 15 — Discuss: How should poems be taught?/"After English Class" by Jean Little

To prepare for future meetings, each of the seven children was given a poetry anthology from which to choose five or six poems that they might like to share with others. I suggested that they not be too hasty with their decisions and that they consider choosing some poems that may initially be confusing.

At the second meeting, children discussed their choices with the group. Each participant read aloud their favorite poems and shared general impressions. Reasons for selecting these poems were as varied as the texts from which they were chosen. Of the choices brought forward by the club members, "Stopping by Woods on a Snowy Evening" initiated the most interest. I've included a transcript of their work with this poem as it serves as a good example of small-group work.

A Small-Group Discussion with the Teacher

Stopping by Woods on a Snowy Evening

Whose woods these are I think I know.
His house is in the village though
He will not see me stopping here
To watch his woods fill up with snow.

My little horse must think it queer
To stop without a farmhouse near
Between the woods and frozen lake
The darkest evening of the year.

He gives his harness bells a shake
To ask if there is some mistake.
The only other sound's the sweep
Of easy wind and downy flake.

The woods are lovely, dark and deep
But I have promises to keep
And miles to go before I sleep,
And miles to go before I sleep.

Robert Frost

Club members began to challenge the opinions of others as they revealed their ideas about the words, images, and stories that the text offered. After their initial speculations, I stepped into the conversation as another member of the group and, although somewhat anxious about how the others might react to my presence, remained in the circle. Upon reflection, I questioned my intervention (more about that later).

The seven club members were: James (J); Jason B. (B); Heidi (H); Georgette (G); Lisa (L); Sunny (S); Teacher (T).

1. B: Maybe he had a bet with someone.
2. T: What would the bet be about?
3. B: That he would stop in the woods.
4. J: That he would walk around the world...
5. S: He's not walking... you see...
6. B: He had to go all through the woods for many miles until he sleeps and if he won he'd get the money and if he didn't he'd have to pay up.

7. H: Or... maybe it's like... maybe someone's gone with him and maybe he got killed and they're remembering what he said.
8. T: ... and James, you said "top secret"... what does that mean?
9. J: I don't know... like he's maybe a spy...
10. T: Sunny, you were trying to say something?
11. S: I don't think he's "top secret"... cause... well, shouldn't it mention something of a hint that he's on a top secret mission?
12. J: I think he was going to see his friends... because he says "his house is in the village" and probably the village is pretty far from there...
13. L: Could I read my poem?
14. T: You want to say something Heidi?
15. H: O.K... like I think it is someone because it says here (reading) "he will not see me stopping here" so I think there's someone that saw him...
16. J: ... and the village is miles away...
17. S: Yeah... he's got promises to keep...
18. G: ... he could be going on a trip...
19. S: ... or maybe someone started to follow him for some reason... that's why he says "he will not see me stopping here."
20. J: Or maybe... maybe somebody in his family is dying.
21. B: ... and he has to go to the village... for his medicine.
22. H: I think the man that's there... like owns that place because it says (reading) "he will not see me here to watch his/*his* (re-reads) woods fill up with snow."
23. B: So it must be God.
24. H: Yeah!
25. S: No... Look!... (reading) "Whose woods there are I think I know/His house is in the village though"... so the person who owns these woods lives in the village.
26. H: Maybe it's private property... that's his property...
27. G: Or somebody is following him!
28. J: Maybe it's in the will that he's going to own the forest when that person dies.
29. G: Yeah!
30. S: Or maybe he's going to a funeral.
31. B: Maybe death is watching him... He says if he stops, he'll die.

32. J: Remember that story that Mr. Swartz read last year...
33. B: Oh yeah... that was awesome!
34. J: What was it?
35. T: "Come Again in the Spring"... where death comes to take a man's life away and they bargain with each other.
36. B: Yeah... that was cool!
37. H: I like this poem... I think that person lives there or like he owns that land because it says "I have a promise to keep," so I think that the person who is talking is following him and he has miles to go before he sleeps... like he has to walk back maybe.
38. T: Could you please read the last verse?
39. H: The whole paragraph?
40. T: the verse... (pointing) the verse...
41. H: (reading) "The woods are lovely, dark and deep/But I have a promise to keep (sic)/And miles to go before I sleep/And miles to go before I sleep."
42. J: But I don't understand one line in the story. "The darkest evening of the year." Why would he go then?
43. H: Maybe it's like you can't see him.
44. B: No... maybe it's because when he has to go... if he doesn't go by then... something bad might happen.
45. J: ... he's a spy...
46. S: That reminds me of a book I read... it's called *The Darkest Day*.
47. J: Who's it by?
48. S: I forget...
49. J: Is it a fantasy?
50. S: Yeah...
51. T: Do you think there's any other meaning to "the darkest night"?
52. B: Or maybe it's like... when there's like the moon... do you know the eclipse... like when the moon disappears?
53. L: I think he's lost.

What, on the evidence of this transcript, did the group achieve? First, one might conclude that since the group was not instructed to talk about the poem in any way, the fear of saying the wrong thing was diminished. Potentially, children's confidences were built up because they could say what they wanted, given the nature of open discussion. This, according to Patrick Dias (1987), author of *Making Sense of Poetry*, serves to develop autonomous readers of poetry.

Second, as the students listened to others, they were made aware of several possibilities of meaning and were exposed to ambiguity rather than closure. James, Sunny, Heidi, Jason, Lisa, and Georgette engaged in a process of shared understanding. The tentativeness of their conversation helped them to find their way to whatever modest discoveries they made and allowed them to modify their points of view as they wished. Douglas Barnes (1976) tells us that a discussion such as this is important because it is a means "by which learners explore the relationship between what they already know and new observations or interpretations which they meet" (p. 81).

As the students discussed the poem they were:
- *speculating* (maybe he had a bet with someone [1]);
- *reasoning* (I think he was going to see his friends because he says his house is in the village and probably the village is pretty far from there [12]);
- *explaining* (... it says here "he will not see me stopping here" so I think that there's someone that saw him [15]);
- *making analogies* (Remember that story last year... [32]);
- *questioning* (I don't understand the line "The darkest evening of the year." Why would he go then? [42]).

For most of this discussion, children concerned themselves with trying to decide on a story of the traveller. They referred to specific lines, which may indicate that they were attempting to infer what Frost was trying to say (e.g., "he's got promises to keep" [17]); "Look... 'His house is in the village though'... so the person who owns these woods lives in the village" [25]). Rarely were attempts made to unravel the complexities suggested by metaphor, although Jason suggested that "maybe death is watching him. He says that if he stops, he'll die" [31]) and later explains that "maybe 'the darkest night' means death" [52]).

The apparent "aimlessness" of such a discussion can be advantageous since the conversation is more "natural" or "real" compared to what might happen when a specific problem is posed for consideration. What the club's discussion illustrates is that there is value in encouraging children to consider their ideas away from what can be the inhibiting influence of teacher opinion and pronouncements. What, then, should a teacher's role be in awakening the ability of children in coming to meaning?

My involvement in this conversation was mainly to ensure that the children kept to the task of discussing the poem. Without my presence, club members may have continued to read their poems aloud without much analysis. In fact, early in the conversation Lisa asked if she could read her poem [13], but I prompted further commitment to the conversation by asking Heidi to offer a comment [14]. I also contributed by providing information (e.g., naming the title of the short story, "Come Again in the Spring," giving instructions to revisit the poem [38]). When James spoke of his confusion about the line, "The darkest evening of the year," I asked, "Do you think there's any meaning to 'the darkest night'?" [51], thereby pointing out the potential of symbolism. However, rather than explaining the "hidden meaning," I suggested to the children that "there's-more-to-this-than-meets-the-eye," thus offering the opportunity for individuals to share speculations.

Such a conversation might be criticized because it lacks the direction that may have occurred had I assigned a topic for the group to discuss (e.g., to collaborate and create a single narrative about the traveller in the woods). For the most part, children tossed out ideas with little attempt to build on them. Given more time, I think they might have been more successful in their analysis. More significant, however, I might have taken a more committed role by shaping the talk, asking questions, and enlarging upon significant points made by the children. The dilemma is a common one: as teachers, we are anxious that children respond in their way to the demands of the literature before them but, at the same time, we feel an obligation to encourage and support them in developing an open style of responding and discussing. Gordon Wells and Gen Ling Chang-Wells (1992) capsulate this dilemma:

> To be maximally effective, the guidance and assistance that the adult gives in such joint problem-solving situations needs to be responsive to the learners' own intentions and understanding and pitched slightly beyond her current level of unaided performance. (p. 29)

Am I abdicating my duty by not accompanying the children in their interpretation of the poem? The question of interpretation, or of meaning, is a sensitive one. How far should we press

64

for deeper meaning or understanding of a poem? Will too much analysis put a stranglehold on children's appreciation of poetry? I suspect it could, and this is why for many "it's grown so complicated" that they don't, as "After English Class" suggests, "bother to stop."

Raising Questions

A while ago, I was visiting Solomon, my eleven-year-old nephew. As we chatted about school, he told be about a surprise poetry test (poetry test?) that his teacher had given his class on William Wordsworth's "Daffodils." Test questions went something like this: *How do you know that the poet was alone in this poem? How is the last verse different from others? To what does the poet compare the daffodils? Where were the daffodils? Explain the meaning of the words "jocund," "pensive," and solitude."*

Solomon didn't do well on his test. For the first question, he answered that the poet was alone because he said, "For oft, when on my couch I lie in "vacant... ."" He got zero for that question because the answer was supposed to be the first line, "I wandered lonely as a cloud." For Solomon, the picture of the poet in a vacant room conveyed loneliness. He also got zero for saying that the daffodils were "high o'er vales and hills" because those were the clouds. Although he wrote that "jocund" meant cheerful; "pensive" deep in thought, and "solitude" being alone, he lost marks because he hadn't written proper sentences.

For homework, Solomon re-wrote the test, making necessary corrections. "What were the correct answers?" I asked my nephew. He explained that his teacher told the class what the answers were when she took up the test.

Instead of exploring the poem through natural talk, curiousity, and revelation, Solomon and his classmates were asked to answer a list of questions that were meant to help them "understand" the poem. What was Solomon's teacher testing? What did she hope to gain by having the students match their answers to hers? With such "tests," it's no wonder that poetry gets a bad name.

Perhaps Solomon's teacher might have had the children respond through art, writing, drama, or talk activities that would lure them into a more significant examination of the poem. Children might have written a journal response where they revealed what they liked, didn't like, or wondered about the poem. They might have prepared a choral dramatization of the poem, created a co-operative picture book, or perhaps role played an interview with the poet.

In lieu of asking questions, the teacher might have conducted a whole-class discussion, inviting children to brainstorm questions *they* had about the poem. Best of all, Solomon's teacher might have structured small-group discussions where the children collaborated to answer their own questions and make sense of Wordsworth's poem.

Children As Questioners

If teachers want to teach children how to engage in thinking, they should teach them how to ask questions. Encouraging children's capacity for questioning helps them become active learners willing to take on new investigations, deal with controversy, and raise questions about questions.

In her article, "The Art of Questioning," Dennis Palmer Wolf (1987) offers two reasons why we need to bother about the questions children ask:

> First, there is a social outcome — students need the face-to-face skill of raising questions with other people: clarity about what they don't understand and want to know; the willingness to ask; the bravery to ask again. Second... being asked and learning to pose strong questions might offer students a deeply held, internal blueprint for inquiry — call it a capacity for question-finding. Question-finding is the ability to go to a poem, painting, piece of music or document, mathematical description, science experiment — and locate a novel direction for investigation. (p. 7)

By honoring questions children ask, we offer them opportunities to take responsibility for their learning and we respect experiences that are available in all learning communities. In most cases, teachers have greater experience, understanding, and insight than children; however, we must remember that each child brings a unique perspective and sense of wonder to any situation.

EVENT 26
. . . .
Questioning ''Daffodils''

Questions will arise in any significant poetry discussion. As children pursued discussion, they began to answer questions for themselves, raising new questions as they unraveled the poem. Though their utterances weren't always stated as questions, they often reflected children's hunches about a poem's meaning.

Daffodils

I wandered lonely as a cloud
That floats on high o'er vales and hills,
When all at once I saw a crowd
A host of golden daffodils,
Beside the lake, beneath the trees
Fluttering and dancing in the breeze,

Continuous as the stars that shine
And twinkle on the milky way,
They stretched in never-ending line
Along the margin of a bay:
Ten thousand saw I at a glance
Tossing their heads in sprightly dance.

The waves beside them, danced, but they
Out-did the sparkling waves in glee:
A poet could not but be gay
In such jocund company!
I gazed — and gazed — but little thought
What wealth the show to me had brought:

For oft, when on my couch I lie
In vacant or in pensive mood,
They flash upon that inward eye
Which is the bliss of solitude;
And then my heart with pleasure fills,
And dances with the daffodils.

William Wordsworth

Each child is given a copy of the poem and forms a group with two or three classmates. You can pose this scenario to the class: "If you had the chance to interview Wordsworth about ''Daffodils,'' what would you ask him about the poem? In your

67

groups, make up a list of questions that you would like to ask."

Once groups complete their lists, they can compare their questions with those of another group. Finally, as a whole class, children can come together to discuss significant questions to ask about "Daffodils." This list was drawn up by my grade five class.

1. Is the place in this poem a real place?
2. Why was this scene so important to this poet?
3. Why is the poem about daffodils and not any other flower?
4. Why does the poet say "a poet could not but be gay?"
5. What does "jocund" mean?
6. Does this poet like being alone?
7. Did he tell anybody about this scene or just write about it?
8. Why does he say "danced" three times?
9. What other parts of nature make him feel bliss?
10. Does the poet enjoy writing about the daffodils more than seeing the daffodils?

Often, the questions children ask are specifically related to the text (Why do you think he compared the daffodils to stars?). At other times, questions may emerge that do not relate specifically to the poem but demonstrate thoughts a child might have about something offered in conversation (Why do we have daffodil days?). At the same time that children work on questioning, they are also making sense of the poem. Children, working with peers, will likely cover items that we would raise and answer questions that we would pose to help them look more closely at the poem.

The following statements were transcribed as a group in my class brainstormed their questions. Statements indicate that the children were doing more than raising questions about "Daffodils." They were:

1. Interpreting
- I don't think he really thought about the importance of the daffodils until he was alone in his house and sitting on the couch.
- He makes the daffodils seem like people by saying they have heads and they dance.

2. Making Guesses
- Jocund must mean something like bright or cheerful.
- I think that he must be very lonely because the only thing that kept him company was the daffodils.

68

3. Revealing Mind Pictures
- If I were going to paint this picture I would put in a thousand yellow dots that look like stars and probably very little green.
- This reminds me of the scene near my cottage with the lakes and hills. We don't have daffodils but there are some purple wildflowers that you see when you drive up to my cottage.

4. Offering Opinions
- I like this poem because he really makes you think how beautiful and important flowers are to cheering you up.
- I like the way he rhymes. For each verse, the first and third line rhyme. The second and fourth line rhyme and the last two lines rhyme. He adds variety to the rhyme.

5. Building Narrative
- I think that this guy is a poet who likes living alone. He probably wanted to write a poem one day and when he couldn't think of anything, he started to wander around.
- I think he is taking his walk on a high hill overlooking the sea, somewhere in England or something. I think he's chosen to live there.

Questions about a text imply that there are answers; children might need a second activity to discuss answers to questions they devise, either in small-group or large-group discussions. I feel, however, that by raising questions, children are involved in a significant context for looking inside and outside the poem. How necessary is it to initiate a further talk experience with the poem? Perhaps questions of the poem and its merits should be allowed to rest inside the reader rather than talking the poem to death.

Certainly, children can uncover meanings (hidden or otherwise) of ''Daffodils'' on their own terms. That is not to say that the teacher cannot draw their attention to some things that they might not have seen, but it is important that she or he be considered a partner in the conversation, one who wonders and asks questions as they do, and not as an expert who has answers to their questions.

EVENT 27
. . . .

Working in Pairs to Raise Questions

This event is similar to the previous event but had students working with a variety of poems to raise questions.

Children, working in pairs, are given a copy of a poem to read. Pairs of children can compile a list of ten to twelve questions that they would ask others about a poem to help them reflect on its meaning.

Once completed, each pair can exchange poems and attempt to answer the questions another pair has devised.

As a final talk activity, each pair can join with another pair to form groups of four. The group can discuss the poems and questions and compare their understandings.

. . . .

Talking About Talking About Poetry: A Reflection

It's time to ask: What do children think is important about talking about poetry? And what do they think is the teacher's role?

In order to have children reflect upon themselves as readers of poetry, I introduced them to Jean Little's poem, ''After English Class'' from *Hey World, Here I Am!* The poem, used to introduce this chapter, provokes us into contemplating our roles as teachers of literature.

As the poem suggests, when a teacher explains everything, children are apt to stop thinking for themselves, hence putting a stop to further enjoyment of poetry. When I ask children to discuss a poem, the dilemma about how much I should intervene continues to bother me. I exposed my dilemma to the class by having them discuss Jean Little's poem.

I didn't have to go further than the first utterances to discover whether the students understood the poem and the notion of response.

James: I think she wrote down ''hidden meanings'' because the first time you look at a poem... some of them you don't really understand, so you have to keep on reading and think to yourself and then after a while it will come to you.

Lisa: I think that when she said that it gets so complicated

70

because a teacher told them there are hidden meanings. I think that the teacher is wrong because everybody has their own meanings. That's why I enjoy these discussions.

Heidi: I think the teacher shouldn't have told them that there was a hidden meaning but they should have found out the meaning by themselves.

As the conversation developed, children talked about the title, riding horses, walking in the woods, teachers, and "Stopping by Woods on a Snowy Evening." Do they understand the notion of personal response? Have they learned anything about teaching and learning poetry?

As the following comments indicate, it seems the children have come a long way as readers of poetry.

Georgette: It's like taste. You might say that this apple tastes good and then the next person who tastes it says "Ugh!.. this is kind of gross." Like everybody has different thoughts...

Lisa: Well, I think if I was her and stopped by the woods every day after English class, and the teacher suddenly tells me the meaning to it... I don't think I'd bother... I'd just go with my own thoughts.

James: The person would think it's one thing and the teacher would talk about another thing and they don't connect together. It doesn't mean it's true just because the teacher says so.

Heidi: Most people I know like things simple. At the beginning of the poem, the woods are simple, but then the teacher comes in and starts talking and makes everything really complicated so that next time she drives by she "won't bother to stop" — or read the poem because it's so complicated.

Perhaps Sunny summarizes it best in the following transcript:

Sunny: If I were the kid in this poem, I wouldn't listen to the teacher.

Georgette: You would listen to her thought but don't take it seriously.

Sunny: The teacher's job is to help you but not give you the whole answer.

James: The teacher points a line out to you...

Sunny: The teacher points you the path, but doesn't take you down it. It's like learning... if the teacher just gives you the

71

answers you won't learn anything but if she tells you what to do, or gives you hints then you might learn it.

In her essay, "Finding Poetry Everywhere," Nancie Atwell (1991) suggests that when teachers give students a full-blown polished analysis of a poem, they tend to think of themselves as deficient readers of poetry because they're unable to achieve instant understanding. Atwell insists that teachers let their students know that we all experience uncertainty at first readings. About teaching poetry, Nancie Atwell has learned to "de-mystify the process of reading a poem so that my students might see how a reader could relish unraveling the difficulties of poetry" (p. 90).

As I set up discussion groups in my class I was very conscious of my role in helping children come to create meaning and hence enjoy poetry. Sometimes I participated in the group discussions; at other times I wasn't present. Sometimes I offered the children an agenda to guide their conversations; at other times the discussions remained open. My intent was to help the children to not be afraid of saying the wrong thing — as David Booth (1988) states, "to enable them to voice their own ideas and provoke them into the surprise of coming to know" (p. 89).

VI

Working As Poets

Writing a Poem

I would love to write a poem
That everyone would love to own
A poem for all to learn by heart
A poem that's a work of art.
But I guess this one isn't it.

L.S.

Poetry Patterns

Sometimes children need shape and pattern to assist them in their struggle to write poems. When they examine the way words are placed on paper by poets (as well as by peers), they might be encouraged to create original poems using patterns they find engaging. Form can give children a sense of control and economy as they write.

Formula poems are usually short and written to specific criteria. Writing poems from a model is often a simple way for some children to begin with poetry as they play with patterns, manipulate words, count syllables, or comply to a specific meter or rhythm. Writing in this way becomes a puzzle for the children to solve as they mold words and release their imaginations.

Having said this, I have some hesitations about teaching the writing of poetry in this fashion. The danger may be that children might see poetry as a paint-by-number exercise where they fill in spaces according to rules. This shouldn't be the case —

children who work as poets should be able to use any colors they wish, any kind of paint they wish, and feel free to go outside the lines.

When I first began teaching, I felt an obligation to "teach poetry" and often turned to some of the formulas that are listed in this section. I was grateful to have Brian Powell's books *Making Poetry* (1973) and *Their Own Special Shape* (1976) to guide me. I think, however, that these formulas should be considered a starting point for teachers and children. On occasion, it's useful to identify poetic forms for children; this may invite them to experiment with models such as haiku or limerick. At other times, such formulas may get in the way of the creative process.

In an art class, I wouldn't think of letting children use only crayons all year. Nor would I be doing my job as a teacher if I gave children a pattern to copy and got twenty-five identical pumpkins, vases, or masks. Likewise, I think children, in order to express themselves through poetry, should have a wide repertoire of word canvases to choose from and be allowed the freedom to bend, shape, ignore, stretch, and invent some of the rules of poem-making.

I offer the following patterns, then, as an appetizer. I hope that those interested in putting poetry into the lives of children will offer a richer main course so that when they're ready to write a poem, they won't think that it must rhyme, have a set number of syllables, or be an acrostic message.

Three-Word Model

This poetry pattern uses a noun, a verb, and adverb (in that order) and lists the three words vertically. The words should make an interesting statement about the topic, the first word in the poem. When all three words begin with the same initial sound, the use of alliteration gives the poem a unifying link.

> raccoons
> rummage
> rowdily
>
> *Alex*

74

Haiku

Haiku presents one simple observation designed to surprise the reader and make him or her contemplate something, usually a specific aspect of nature.

A haiku tries to convey a mood or feeling in a powerful way with few words. Seventeen syllables in length, it follows the pattern of three lines of five, seven, and five syllables.

by a frozen lake
a jay darts to take quick flight
blue sky flash on ice

Christi

Cinquain

One cinquain model is a shape poem composed of five lines. Each line has a purpose and can follow a word or syllable count.

Line 1: one word, naming the subject
Line 2: two adjectives describing the subject
Line 3: three additional adjectives describing the subject
Line 4: four words telling something about the subject
Line 5: line 1 is repeated

Werewolf
Scary, Hairy
Howling Yowling Prowling
Beware the Stalker's Bite
Werewolf

Erica

Word Association

Children can brainstorm a list of words or expressions that they associate with an assigned topic or title. As children's comments are recorded to form a list, a word association poem is created.

Children can list words and then reshape the list by eliminating, adding, or combining words on a single line, repeating words, or arranging lines into an interesting poetic form. Children, as a group, can share ideas and build a co-operative poem, as these grade seven children did.

Adolescence

changing
excited, bored
difficult, sporadic, volatile
and of course versatile
problem?
          no problem
problems
play
    work
play
difficult (sometimes)
no longer a child (sometimes)
restricted
challenged, challenging
youthful, exhilarating
growing, growing, growing
leave me alone
who am I?

Rebecca, Jacqui, Johanne, Trevor

Eight-Word Rhyming Poem

In this four-line poem, the second and fourth line rhyme. Each line consists of two words.

Cat

slithering, slinking
darting high
under foot
sliding by

                    Sarah

Limerick

The limerick, a five-line poem, follows a definite rhyme scheme and rhythm pattern.
Lines 1, 2, and 5 rhyme
Lines 1, 2, and 5 have three strong beats
Lines 3 and 4 rhyme
Lines 3 and 4 have two strong beats.

A limerick is usually a nonsense poem.
Line 1 tells something about the subjects, perhaps stating where she or he is from
Line 2 describes the person or some action
Lines 3 and 4 continue the idea about the subject mentioned in line 2
Line 5 gives a funny or unexpected ending.

> There was an Old Man with a beard,
> who said, "It is just as I feard! —
> Two owls and a hen,
> Four larks and a wren
> Have all built their nests in my beard!
>
> *Edward Lear*

Simile Structure

For this short poem, children don't reveal their subject until the final line. Beginning lines tell something about the subject by using similes to describe some aspect of the subject.
Line 1: simile image
Line 2: simile image
Line 3: simile image(s)
Line 4: names two or three actions
Line 5: names the subject

> Ears like fans flapping the breeze
> Legs like forest stumps
> Tail like a whip, nose like a hose
> He waddles, he snorts, he trumpets
> Elephant
>
> *Brian*

Closed Couplet

A couplet is two lines that rhyme, one after the other, usually equal in length. When one couplet makes a complete poem it is called a "closed couplet."

> If I were a bird and a bird was me
> He'd be writing this poem and I'd be up a tree
>
> *L.S.*

77

Acrostic Poem

Acrostic poems look something like a simple crossword puzzle, and use a person or place name as a topic. For every letter in the word, children can think of a word or group of words that tell about the topic.

D anger to the
E nvironment and
A tmosphere
R escue please

W orld problem with
O zone
R evive
L ove please and
D iscover our dear world

Taylor

List Poem

List poems are fun to write. Once a topic or title is chosen, children can brainstorm a list of ideas that they associate with the topic. What transforms an ordinary list into a poem is a linking factor such as adjectives only, verbs only, or alliterative words. The following list poem is linked by alphabet, names, and adjectives that end in the same syllable and alliterative pairs.

3:10 Friday Afternoon

Ann's angry
Bob's busy
Carl's crazy
Daisy's dizzy
Edna's edgy
Fiona's fussy
Gail's giggly
Harry's happy
Izzy's itchy
Jason's jiggly
Karim's counting the seconds
Liza's lazy
Mona's mopy

Ned's needy
  Olga's out of line
Petra's perky
Quincy's quirky
Ryan's ready
Sunny's steady
Tina's tingly
Una's uppity
Verna's vervy
Willy's wily
Xavier's facing the wrong
direction
Yona's yappy
Zelda's zzzzzzzzzz

     Sunil, Matthew, Ryan, James

Finding Poems Here and There

Sometimes children transform words that haven't been written as poems into poems. Using this strategy, they can find poems in ordinary, and not so ordinary, places. By rearranging, adding, and repeating words, and by creating a shape in which to fit words, they can transform novel excerpts, instructions, messages, newspaper articles, recipes, and conversations — any place where words are found — into poems.

EVENT **28**
. . . .
Finding Poems in the News

Newspaper headlines and accompanying articles are a convenient source for making poems. For a two-week period, an intermediate-level class subscribed to a local newspaper for a media study. When they were finished with the newspapers, I brought them to our class to help my students uncover poems in yesterday's news.

Children can select a short article that interests them from an old newspaper or magazine. They can underline words or phrases they feel were important to the article using a highlighter. Children can then copy the words they underlined on a piece

79

of paper, arranging the phrases into a poem by experimenting with line breaks and white spaces. Children can be encouraged to eliminate, add or repeat words, and to work with friends who can help edit their work. When all children are comfortable with their poem, they can paste it on a piece of paper or card and decorate it to match the mood of their poem.

EVENT 29
· · · · · · · · · · · ·
Finding Poems in Novels

Some prose is so rhythmic or descriptive that it could be written as free verse. Look at this example that Georgette adapted from Kevin Henkes wonderful novel, Words of Stone.

> *Her fingers*
> *moved like dancers*
> *pushing and pulling*
> *bringing a garden to life*
> *with thread.*

To experiment with free verse poetry, ask the children to select one or two lines from a novel they are reading that they think paint a picture or use words in an interesting way. Children can copy the sentence(s) onto a piece of paper and play with line breaks and white spaces to re-write the text as a free verse poem. Encourage children to change words or make additions they think necessary.

EVENT 30
· · · · · · · · · · · ·
Finding Poems in First Lines

Often poetry anthologies are accompanied by an index of first lines. On one occasion, I used selections from an index to prompt the students to write a poem based on a first line of a published poem. Here are some examples from A Year Full of Poems *that proved useful for this activity.*

- *Among the busy streets*
- *Before the paling of the stars*
- *Have you ever heard the sun in the sky*

- *I stood beside a hill*
- *Spring is*
- *Summer sun bakes*

Children can choose a first line of a poem that they like or find challenging. They can then write a poem of their choice, structured or free verse. When the children are finished with their poem, they can exchange them with classmates. Here is Samuel's poem, based on the first line, ''Spring's first.''

EVENT 31
. . . .

Finding Poems in Conversations

Sometimes children's speech is full of poetry. Unless the opportunity is taken to preserve these expressions in print, the poetry can easily escape.

Children can discuss the idea that poetry does not have to spring from print, that we often sprinkle conversations with words that can be written poetically. To give children an idea of how this can be done, listen carefully as they speak. Pick a sentence or sentence fragment that could be converted and bring it to the children's attention.

Children can be encouraged to listen to themselves in ordinary conversation. When they say something in an unusual way, invite them to write it down to discover the uniqueness of the way they express themselves. In this way, notebooks can become a significant medium for having children reflect on their words, their voices, and the episodes of their lives.

As one example, Jamie was exasperated with his writing and at the end of the day yelled out, "I don't want to do a poem/I want to go home." As his final copy demonstrates, Jamie produced a short piece that included rhyme, repetition, showed an understanding of free verse form, and used a variety of print sizes to emphasize his thoughts.

EVENT 32
. . . .
Borrowing from the Poets

Children sometimes write poems that are modelled on those that have been introduced to the classroom or that they have encountered in poetry collections. Poems that work best for this activity have a distinct rhyme scheme or shape.

I challenged my class to create an original piece using the rhyme and rhythm of poems such as "Clickbeetle" by Mary Ann Hoberman, "This Is My Rock" by David McCord, and "Hurray!" by Dr. Fitzhugh Dodson. When children borrow from poets, they are lured into re-visiting the original poem and come to terms with how rhyme and form work together. Once they have grasped these elements, they are asked to use a new word palette to create an original piece.

A lesson where children create an original piece of writing patterned on a specific source, for example, Bill Martin Jr.'s popular "Brown Bear, Brown Bear," can provide a good start for children's writing. To begin, children can work as a whole class. When they have developed some confidence with the technique, they can work on their own or with a partner to create additional verses.

82

I have to write a
poem
But I
want
go
home
I want to go home
But I have to
do A POEM

by
Jamie Boot

The following suggestions may be useful for patterning poems:
- Children should have the opportunity to read the poem aloud several times using a variety of choral techniques.
- The procedure of patterning can be demonstrated with the whole class. By starting with the cloze technique, children see how they can replace words in the original poem.

- Children can work with one or two friends so that they can brainstorm and negotiate ideas. Patterning thus becomes a significant problem-solving activity.
- When children think they have finished with the poem, they can be encouraged to read it aloud (or have someone else read it aloud) and consider whether they've captured the rhythm and rhyme scheme of the original poem.
- Children should be encouraged to add, eliminate, or substitute words in their first drafts.
- Children should realize that it's alright to go outside the pattern and invent their own if they have trouble with rhyming or fitting the meter of the original poem.

Those familiar with Jack Prelutsky's "Bleezer's Ice Cream Store" can recognize where Alan and Jeffrey got their idea for this poem.

> Miss Amanda Wurger
> Bought a barbecued hamburger
> A great big super dooper
> It was a sixty seven scooper
> And on it she put..
>
> onions, relish, tomatoes ripe
> mustard, lettuce, a ketchup stripe
> milk and eggs, butter and beans
> she also added some lettuce greens
> crispy chips and chocolate mint
> cotton candy and peppermint
> orange, lime and sour lemon
> raspberry tart, watermelon
> maple walnut, raisin rum
> tutti frutti bubble gum
>
> Amanda was full
> Didn't want any more
> She paid her bill
> And left the store
>
> *Alan and Jeffrey*

EVENT **33**
· · · · · · · · · · · ·

Finding Poems in Strange Places

Wherever words are found, so are poems. A list of words, a sentence, or a phrase can be manipulated into a rhyming or free verse poem by changing its original shape.

This list suggests places that poems were uncovered in Room 203.

- *billboards*
- *magazine advertisements*
- *newspaper headlines*
- *labels*
- *menus*
- *titles*
- *recipes*
- *dictionaries*
- *atlases*
- *road signs*
- *comics*
- *lists*
- *messages*
- *names*
- *announcements*
- *graffiti*
- *manuals*
- *instructions*
- *letters*
- *postcards*

Ask the children to select one of these items and peruse it for interesting language. They can select a fragment and use it as a base to write a poem. Poems can be decorated and displayed with other poems originating from the source (e.g., dictionary poems, announcement poems).

· · · · · · · · · · · ·

Publishing Our Poems

Because she knows all to well the work it takes to be considered a poet, Myra Cohn Livingston (1990) has never told children that they are poets. Livingston writes, "Are we so afraid to tell our children that they are not poets, that they are only beginning to learn something of the craft, but that if they wish, through work and re-writing, they may eventually achieve something of which they will be proud?" (p. 38)

When I read poems written by children in reference books such as *Lasting Impressions, For the Good of the Earth and Sun,* and *Sunrise and Songs,* I am surprised and stimulated by their power and wonder what went behind the formulation and transcription of putting pencil to paper. What did the poem look like in the beginning? How many versions preceded the published poem? Where did the child get the seed to plant a poem? What happened in the child's life that made him or her share that thought? Why did she or he choose the poetic form? Did she or he intend to write a poem? How did the teacher intervene with the poetry-writing process?

For Myra Cohn Livingston, teaching poetry demands involvement on the part of the teacher, a commitment to elicit a child's feelings or experiences and help him or her to write something that may approach, but not yet be, a poem.

While children may not be poets, they share many of the creative qualities that poets possess. When children play with words to express their ideas and feelings, they behave like poets. Of course, children struggle to use poetic language effectively, to write in what can be considered "acceptable" poetic form, to convey an emotion or an image artistically. Often, however, it is the simplicity of their prose that allows children to come to a poetic sensibility.

Here are three basic approaches to have children write as poets.

1. Give them patterns and structures on which to hang their ideas.

> Beautiful jar on the counter
>   What's inside you?
> Maybe a cookie
>   maybe not
> Maybe a butterfly
>   maybe not
> Maybe a bird
>   maybe not
> Maybe a thought
>   maybe not
> Beautiful jar on the counter
>   What's inside you?
>
> *Karrie*

2. Have them use poems as forms for expressing their thoughts and feelings.

> the earth is like a diamond
> so perfect
> so precious
> the earth is like a diamond
> so hard to break

86

but we are earth miners
and we are breaking it

if the diamond breaks
only 8 of the jewels
remain
there will be no diamond

Matthew

3. Restructure what they have written into a more poetic frame.

My friend he was
He moved.
            I moved
I never heard from him
again.
Goodbye, my friend
Goodbye.

Shawn

There is so much more to the act of writing than putting words on a page. I agree with Amy McClure (1990) when she says that poems are never viewed as finished. She compares the writing process to baking bread: "kneading, punching it down, leaving it alone, then kneading some more until satisfied that a unique statement has been made" (p. 36).

Like any piece of writing that is going to be revised, lines are cut out, words are changed, spelling errors are corrected, and new perspectives are taken. Poetry is a matter of seeking out the best word or words, the best place to begin or end a line, and the best way of touching the mind and heart.

In McClure's book *Sunrise and Songs*, one grade three student writes:

Writing a poem
Is like piloting a plane
If it's not flying smoothly,
Throw out the excess baggage.

It is the teacher's job to recognize the potential of the piece and assist the child in the refining and revising processes. Georgia Heard (1989) claims that the crucial element in responding to any-one's poetry is the sense of being listened to and understood.

87

When she truly listened, Heard said, she "started to teach the writer of the poems, not the poems themselves" (p. 39). In this way, Heard is teaching each student according to where she or he is as a writer.

As I inspect children's poems, I am able to recognize the processes that went into making their poems. Their writing of poetry has been nurtured by reading and listening to poetry. We have discussed words in poems, considered the feelings that a poem has elicited, and looked carefully at shapes, images, and surprises in the works of great poets.

EVENT 34
. . . .
Children Publishing Poems

In the latter part of the year, I purchased hardbound books with twenty-four blank pages and gave one to each child to publish poems that they wrote throughout the year. Children selected poems for publication, reviewing and revising their work before entering the poems in their books.

To introduce their books, suggest that children choose a poem from a favorite poet. Reviewing poems of the day that the class has experienced is one way to jog children's memories of the poets they have met in the class. They can write this poem on the first page of their book and illustrate it. A single line or a few words extracted from that poem can serve as the title of their personal collections.

For their anthologies, ask the children to review poems that they wrote in their notebooks. Poems can be in response to a theme, a novel or a poem, or depicting a personal experience. Children can select the poems they feel best represent their work and copy them in their book. If they wish, they can illustrate some or all of the poems.

One of Lindsay's favorites was "There's a Book Inside my Head," which she included in her poetry book.

There's a book inside my head
That needs to be read
It will tell my mysteries
and my laughters
follow me and
I will read my stories
for you!!!

Ha Ha Ha
Ha Ha Ha
Ha

EVENT 35

Assembling a Class Anthology of Student-Authored Poems

In June, Room 203 assembled an anthology of poems written by class members. Each child chose a favorite poem and submitted it as his or her entry to the publication. Most poems emerged from children's personal anthologies. Children also illustrated their poems.

Publishing a class anthology is a significant vehicle for sharing work with an audience. Although a theme can be useful for linking poems, you can compile an anthology that is not shaped by a focus.

89

Ask each child to select one poem that she or he has written and would like included in the anthology. Encourage children to make at least one change to their poems — adding or changing a word, eliminating something that didn't work, or rearranging the form. Once they are comfortable with the final product, children can decide on an appropriate style of illustration — soft (watercolor), hard (ink), and so on.

When all children have finished, their work can be compiled in book form and a copy made for each child in the class. The covers of the grade three and grade five anthologies are shown here.

VII

Poems for Drama

Poems

A poem is a magical boat to ride
in a sea of words with a rhyming tide.
It takes us from some hum-drum shore
to places we never have been before —
shimmering islands of sensation
captured by imagination.
New lands wait for us to sight,
so climb aboard! The wind is right.
Rocking rhythms will take us along
to the rising crest of a noteless song.

Bobbi Katz

A Drama Structure with a Nursery Rhyme

Years ago, I participated in a workshop with Bob Barton. The experience taught me much about organizing drama as a context for inquiry, narration, and role playing. Bob, using a piece of text of about thirty words, quickly had participants raising questions and hypothesizing stories as they attempted to solve the mystery within the two-sentence story he offered.

I am grateful to Bob Barton for this simple structure and have used variations of it with a number of sources. Perhaps because they are short or because they feature peaks of a narrative, I find that nursery rhymes offer a rich springboard for storytelling and dramatic exploration.

Hector Protector was dressed all in green
Hector Protector was sent to the Queen
The Queen did not like him
Nor more did the King
So Hector Protector was sent back again.

Exploring a Nursery Rhyme

- Experiencing the text: Choral speaking techniques.
- Literal interpretation: What facts do we know?
- Hypothesizing: What guesses can you make about the story?
- Inquiry: What questions do you have about this event?
  - Option 1: Brainstorm questions orally with a partner or in a small group.
  - Option 2: Brainstorm questions with a partner or small group and record them on a chart.
  - Option 3: Brainstorm, as a class, a list of questions that concern us (can be oral or recorded). Note: Questions can be promoted in a role-playing interview situation. This strategy, however, allows the group to slow the drama and practise questioning skills.
- Setting the context: Who would you like to speak about this event? (I usually withhold the protagonist, e.g., Hector Protector.)
- Interviewing: What stories can we learn? Before conducting the interview, discuss with the class who might be asking questions. Why?
  - Option 1: Whole class interviews various characters in turn.
  - Option 2: Interviews are conducted in pairs or small-group situations.
  - Option 3: Children can move from character to character, who are seated around the room.

92

Exploring a Nursery Rhyme (cont'd)

- Storytelling: Children, in groups, discuss what information they think the story is, incorporating from their interviews.
- Deepening: Consider in what space and time and with which characters will we experience the story. What problem(s) need to be solved? What strategies will we choose (interview, improvisation, storytelling, mime, tableau, writing — diary, letter, document)?

Ten Ways of Working with Nursery Rhymes

There are a number of ways you can employ nursery rhymes as vehicles for language and drama exploration. The ten suggestions outlined here will provide a base for exploring nursery rhymes in your classroom.

1. Children, in groups, can use a nursery rhyme to *practise choral reading techniques*. They should consider the use of movement, song, sound effects, instruments, props, and so on. If each group is given the same rhythm, groups can compare how rhymes are presented (each will be different).

   Children can *create a class audio tape* of nursery rhymes, with some children reading a poem alone, with a partner, or in small groups. Several poems can be read by the whole class.

2. Children can *review nursery rhyme anthologies* (see pg. 123) and compare how various artists have illustrated the same rhyme. They can also create a nursery rhyme anthology, with each child illustrating one verse (magazine pictures are a possible source of illustration).

3. Children, in pairs or in small groups, can role play the part of journalists *interviewing* nursery rhyme characters. Each child should have an opportunity to role play the part of a nursery rhyme character. Children can also write a newspaper article that features the events of one rhyme.

4. Children can *write a sequel* to a rhyme by creating one or more

93

verses, using the same rhyme scheme as the original verse. Once children have prepared the verse(s), they can decide how to *present* it chorally.

5. Children can *prepare questions* for a nursery rhyme trivia quiz, which tests participants' knowledge of characters and details of nursery rhymes.

6. Children can use nursery rhymes for *storytelling*. They can include details that might have happened before or after events described in the rhyme. Children can brainstorm a list of people who might be telling the story. In pairs, they can conduct interviews with each other to discover "The true story of... ." These stories could then be written up.

7. Children can *have a Mother Goose Day*, perhaps dressing in costume. For their celebration, children might include a puppet play, a mural, written stories and poems, drawings, plasticine models, choral presentations, and snacks.

8. Using *vocabulary* from nursery rhymes, children can create a spelling game, word search, or crossword puzzle for others to solve.

9. Using two or three nursery rhymes, children can *create a chart* to compare rhymes (rhyme scheme, characters, length, colors, action, words, etc.).

    As an alternative activity, children could be given a number of nursery rhymes and decide which rhymes can be classified together. Children can invent as many categories as they feel necessary.

10. Children can *combine two nursery rhymes*. Working in groups of four (two pairs), children can decide how the two rhymes can be read together (e.g., simultaneously, alternating lines, repeating lines).

They can *create a short improvisation* that features characters from rhymes (e.g., what would happen if the characters from each rhyme met).

A Drama Exploration with a Poem

When children participate in role-playing and improvisation activities using poems, they are working inside the poem to bring meaning to it. Using a poem as a source, the class can explore issues and ideas embedded in the poem, thus promoting a wider perception of the poet's images, words, and thoughts.

94

When a teacher chooses to use poems for drama, she or he can choose activities where the children enact incidents from the poem, extend its action, elaborate on its concepts, or invent a drama from the details of the poem. Role playing offers an important opportunity for children to develop their oral interpretation skills, as well as providing a context for discussion, questioning, retelling, storytelling, and improvisation.

EVENT 36
· · · · · · · · · · ·

Exploring "The Voice"

This event details activities that both the grade three and five classes experienced with the poem, "The Voice." The lesson was implemented over a three-day period, with each session lasting sixty to ninety minutes. This structure demonstrates one way of working inside and outside the poem, in role and out, and facilitates strategies for talking, writing, and visual arts.

The Voice

As I sat in the gloaming
I heard a voice say,
Weep no more, sigh no more;
Come, come away!

It was dusk at the window;
From down in the street
No rumble of carts came,
No passing of feet.

I sat very still,
Too frightened to play;
And again the voice called me,
Little boy, come away!

Dark, darker it grew;
Stars came out, and the moon
Shone clear through the glass
The carpet upon.

I listened and listened;
But no more would it say —

The voice that had called me,
Come, Come away!

Walter de la Mare

Session One

Phase 1:
Before listening to the poem, children can predict what they think
the voice is (e.g., male, female, young, old).

Phase 2:
The class can brainstorm a list of questions that they have about
"The Voice" (e.g., who is listening to the voice, how loud is
the voice).

Phase 3:
Copies of the poem can be distributed to the children. They can
read it privately and record a response by raising a question or
offering an opinion about the poem.

Phase 4:
Children, as a class, can share some of the comments they have
written and discuss the poem. Were original questions answered?
What further questions were raised? Questions can be listed on
a piece of chart paper; children can discuss how some of the questions can be answered through drama work.

Phase 5:
The class can experiment with ways of reading the poem aloud.
They can begin by reading the part of the voice (italics) while
the teacher reads the rest of the poem. Parts can then be reversed.
Children can also experiment with types of voices (e.g., sad,
frightened, computer-like).

Phase 6:
The class can stand as a group, imagining that they are stand-
ing outside the window of the house in which the boy sat. On
a signal, children can offer suggestions of what they saw in the
room by describing the furniture, the boy's clothing, and so on.

Session Two

Phase 7:
This phase has children build a context for the work. As a class, children can build a story about the family (e.g., time period, size of family).

Phase 8:
The teacher can assume the role of the mother of the little boy, conducting an interview that might have taken place between the boy and his mother. Collectively, the children can role play the part of the boy. Questioning children about the boy is an effective way to elicit their thoughts on the appearance of the voice.

Phase 9:
The teacher can role play the boy; the class, the voice. A line can be drawn that would represent the door that separated the boy from the voice. Children can be reminded that the boy never saw the voice, and so they must pretend that they can't see each other as the conversation takes place.

Session Three

Phase 10:
Children can work in small groups to discuss what they thought was the story of "The Voice" in order to answer some of the questions they may have raised earlier (e.g., is it dangerous? where did it want to take the child?).

Phase 11:
Children can be told that the voice might have visited other households in the community. The class can hold a meeting where all community members can share their experiences with the voice.

Extensions

1. Children, in small groups, can write a fifth stanza for "The Voice" that continues Walter de la Mare's poem. Before writing their verses, children should revisit the poem chorally to better grasp the rhythm and rhyme scheme. By combining verses that have been written in the class, groups can collaborate to make an original poem.

2. Children, working in pairs or threes, can discuss the conversation that might have taken place had the voice returned. They can improvise conversations between the voice and the boy or other characters.
3. Children can create a drawing that would represent the character of the voice. Characters could write a description and short autobiography of the the voice to accompany their drawings, providing information that would explain its story.
4. Using the information from the drama, children can write a story about the appearance of the voice. They may wish to tell the story through a letter, diary entry, or newspaper article.
5. Children can create a dance drama that tells the story of the voice, that is, tell the story in movement accompanied by a fitting piece of music.

· · · · · · · · · · ·

Structuring Drama with Poems

The class spent a day investigating poems in Eloise Greenfield's anthology, *Night on Neighborhood Street*. In this collection, Greenfield tells the stories of a little boy yearning for a friend who has moved away, an older sister tucking her little sister in bed, and a household where everyone enjoys ''Fambly Time.'' Though we meet such hardened characters as a father who is out of work and a drug seller that the children steer away from, we also learn about jokes, the sound of horns, gospel singing, hugs, and family kisses. In each of the poems in this collection, Greenfield captures a sense of strength that is derived from relationships and the community that many readers can recognize.

EVENT 37
· · · · · · · · · · ·
A Day with *Night on Neighborhood Street*

The following outline provides a structure of the day's events that brought the children to Neighborhood Street *and* Neighborhood Street *to the children. A similar structure could be used with other poems about people, written by different poets or by a single poet.*

98

Children can imagine that these characters live on the same street, and make some decisions about the ways that these characters are related or connected.

Whole-Class Discussion

Begin by discussing the title of the anthology and making guesses about scenes that Eloise Greenfield might have described in her poems. After glancing briefly at the illustrations, children can talk about the types of characters they expect to meet and what their stories might be. You can discuss with them how Jan Spivey Gilchrest's illustrations compliment the text.

The first poem of the anthology, *Neighborhood Street*, gives a sense of the community that the reader will encounter. You can read aloud this poem to the children as they look at the illustrations. Children discuss both the poems and the street scenes illustrated. They can discuss, in small groups, what the scenes make them think of.

Choral Speaking in Small Groups

Children can form groups of two or three. Each group is given a copy of a single poem from the anthology and asked to prepare a choral dramatization of the poem — they assign parts among themselves. Children can be encouraged to experiment with voices, add sounds and movements, and find an appropriate position for presenting the poem.

Forty-five minutes should be sufficient time for most children to rehearse the presentation and share their work with one another. Children can watch each other's work, not only for the way they present the poem aloud, but also to discover information about people and places on the street.

Each group will present its poem differently. Though children could likely use more time to polish their presentation, the activity serves the purpose of having them look inside the poem as they work together to solve the problem of presentation.

Storytelling

Children can discuss what they know about the characters and their feelings by listening to the poems. They are now ready to develop some of the stories about these characters.

99

(a) Creating a Map of Neighborhood Street

A large outline of a street can be sketched onto the blackboard. In order to understand more about Neighborhood Street, children can be asked to come to the board and draw houses and buildings on the street. As each child marks a building on the drawing, she or he can do so in the role of one of Greenfield's characters. When I did this activity with my class, I questioned each child as if I were a stranger to the street. Children, in role, explain who lives there, how long they've lived there, what jobs the family has, and give their impression about living on the street. As the activity develops, children have the opportunity to introduce new characters to the street.

When the map is complete, children can reflect on what they know about Neighborhood Street. In our class, we decided that it was a rather poor community, but a happy one. There was concern about a stranger who was trying to sell drugs to children—the parents were worried about their children's safety. Most wanted to move from Neighborhood Street but couldn't afford to. Mothers and fathers worked hard and spent as much time with their children as they could. Some people had lived on Neighborhood Street their whole lives, others had moved there recently.

(b) Designing a Room

Children can work in the same groups they formed for their choral presentations. Using a large sheet of chart paper, children can design a room for the character in their poem. By creating this drawing, children are able to step into the shoes of the character to better consider what his or her life is like on Neighborhood Street.

Drawings can be displayed. Children can examine one another's drawings and attempt to uncover information about the characters by looking at a drawing of their bedrooms and the things in it.

Improvisation

(a) The Meeting

One of Greenfield's poems, ''The Meeting,'' describes the time when the people on Neighborhood Street get together to talk things out. For a whole-group improvisation, children can create one of these meetings in the classroom. Some students can become the people in the poems, while others role play the part of a friend or relative of that person. Others can invent new characters (a teacher at the local school, the owner of a variety store) that could live on Neighborhood Street.

Prior to the drama, children can consider what problems the community might gather to meet about, for example:

- A new person has moved to Neighborhood Street; residents form a welcoming party to introduce themselves.
- City Hall wants to put a new community center at the end of Neighborhood Street and is interested in hearing citizens' opinions about what the center should offer and whether they think it's a good idea.
- City Hall wants to tear down the houses on the street to build condominiums.
- Neighborhood people decide to do something about the house that's been vacant for years, i.e., "The House with the Wooden Windows."
- Two neighbors disagree about damage that's been done to their property; the community gathers to help them solve the problem.
- A drug seller appears from time to time on Neighborhood Street.

The class can pick one of these scenarios to explore or make up a new scenario. In role, children can volunteer relevant information and make recommendations.

(b) The Future of Neighborhood Street

As a final drama activity, children can work in small groups to create a frozen tableau to show what they think Neighborhood Street will look like in twenty years.

As children work on their tableaux, they can prepare to recite a phrase or one or two lines of Eloise Greenfield's poetry that would serve as a link to the past.

As the tableaux are presented, each child can recite excerpts from the poems they read earlier in the day to show what the characters might have been thinking.

A final discussion can explore what the future holds for Neighborhood Street and what changes might happen to the various members of the community.

Writing Poems

Children, working alone, can compose a poem describing a character (one of Greenfield's or an invented character) on Neighborhood Street, writing from the point of view of the character or in the third person, as Eloise Greenfield did.

Children will have time to prepare a draft copy of their poems; over the next few days, they can work to prepare a published copy of the poem and accompanying illustrations. We assembled our poems into a class anthology entitled *Another Night on Neighborhood Street*, which served as a sequel to Eloise Greenfield's collection.

Possible Extensions with *Night on Neighborhood Street*

- Children can write a diary entry of one of Greenfield's characters, describing a typical day in his or her life.
- A television news program is going to prepare a documentary about life in the city. Children can create a videotape (real or fictitious) that tells others what life on Neighborhood Street is like.
- Using the information from the poems, children can improvise a scene that would bring the character to life. For instance, how would Darnell's parents handle his nighttime fears? How could Juma persuade his father to stay up late?
- The children of Neighborhood Street have grown up. What stories will they tell their children or grandchildren? Children can tell these stories orally in small groups or record them.
- Children can write a poem that is patterned on one of Eloise Greenfield's poems that tells about an episode or a person from their own family or community.

VIII

Poems Up Close

Poems are like barbecued steaks
   Sometimes tender
   Sometimes juicy
   Sometimes well done
How do you like yours?
Me?
I like mine with
   lots of spice
   lots of flavour
   lots of meat
   lots to savour.

Liza Taylor, grade 5

What Is a Poem?

In *The Place My Words Are Looking For*, anthologist, Paul B. Janeczko (1990) collects poems, memories, and anecdotes of thirty-nine leading poets for young people. Here is a sample of poetry definitions these poets offered.

For me poetry has always been a way of paying attention to the world.
Naomi Shihab Nye

Writing poems can be a way of pinning down a dream (almost); capturing a moment, a memory, a happening; and at the same time, it's a way of sorting out your thoughts and feelings. Sometimes the words tell you what you didn't know you knew.

Lillian Morrison

Talk with a little luck in it, that's what poetry is — just let the words

take you where you want to go. You'll be invited; things will happen in your life, you will have more in it than other people's lives.
William Stafford

There is something about poems that is like loving children: They keep returning home and singing to you all your life.
Felice Holman

More definitions are suggested by dozens of favorite poets, as well as those writing about the teaching of poetry. If these writers challenge themselves to find an appropriate definition of poetry, how much more difficult is it for children to explain?

EVENT 38

Defining Poetry

This event had children explore the meaning of the word "poem," which is not a simple task. They worked independently and in small groups using words and symbols to come up with a number of definitions of the word "poem," both in word and picture definitions.

Children can be asked to imagine that they are dictionary editors. As editors, they must define the word "poem." Functions of a poem and what it looks like in comparison to prose should be considered. Children can begin this activity by writing, in twenty-five words or less, their definition of "poem." Here are some samples from my class.

Ryan: A poem is something short but meaningful.

Greg: Poems can rhyme or don't have to. It's a list of words that make sense.

Shannon: A poem is words that do not have to make sense.

James: A poem is like a train entering a tunnel. First there is the dark but you know that there is going to be a light at the end of the tunnel.

Still in their role of dictionary editors, children can work in small groups to compare their definitions. Each group negotiates ideas and devises a new definition of the word by combining and revising personal definitions.

Next, children write the definition in *exactly* twenty-five words.

The specific number is a challenge for children; they must select words carefully as they search for the most meaningful explanation of the word, as these samples from my class indicate.
Group 1:
A poem is a short story or explanation where you put your imagination and different feelings together in words to express your dreams and yourself.
Group 2:
A poem is... A word picture made by breaking up sentences and paragraphs. You have to read a poem carefully because it can turn your whole thought around.
Group 3:
A poem is a way of talking on paper to express your feelings. When you read a poem it becomes a painting in your head.

As a final activity, children can be challenged to present their definitions using *picture symbols* only. Inform them that the dictionary company doesn't allow words — visual images have to explain the meaning of "poem."

Once children prepare a rough sketch, give them a blank slide called "Write On Slides" available from camera equipment stores and a pencil to present their illustration. They can discuss, as a whole class, the slides and determine if one or more is suitable. If not, they can combine aspects of several slides to create one that defines the word "poem" in symbols.

These activities prompt discussion of how a poem can serve many purposes. By explaining what a poem is, children realize that it does not have to rhyme, that it can take different shapes, and that poems are written for different reasons. A poem can tell a story, prompt a thought or image, or entertain or stimulate a particular mood.

. . . .

In their definitions of poetry, children write that poetry matters because it is about "stories," "messages," and "entertainment." For Ricky, poetry is about "figuring out what words mean"; for Billy, "making paragraphs into short sentences"; for Charlene, another way of sending "mind messages to someone."

It is one thing to tell children that poetry matters and quite another to immerse them in poetry so that they can come to understand the significance a poem might have in shaping our thoughts and tapping our emotions.

Why Poetry Matters: The Children's Voices

To help the children look closer at poetry, I invited them to work in small groups to consider why poetry matters and brainstorm criteria that they felt make a poem good to read. The following list reveals how one group of grade three children came to terms with the significance of poetry.

What Makes a Poem Good
by Bobbi, Samantha and Lindsay

1. A good poem makes you think of all the things that you've done (and things you haven't done).
2. A good poem puts pictures in your head. It's like turning a television on in your brain.
3. When you finish reading a good poem, it gives you feelings.
4. A poem is good when the rhymes are fun to read aloud. You can change your voice.
5. A good poem makes you think of other poems.
6. A good poem has pictures that help you understand the poem better when you're a little kid.
7. A poem is good if it doesn't go too fast.
8. The way the poet plays around with the words makes a poem good.
9. A poem is good when you read it silently and want to be in the poem.
10. A poem is good... when you understand it.

What Poetry Means to Me: A Questionnaire

The following questionnaire can be used with your students to have them reflect on the significance of poetry in their lives. Responses may reveal how much children appreciate poetry or indicate their familiarity with the genre. It might be interesting to implement a questionnaire such as this at the beginning of the year and perhaps at the end of the year.

Once children have answered the questions, it is best to have them work in small groups to compare responses and discover their different attitudes.

1. Here are the names of some poets I know

_____

2. A poem I particularly like is

_____

3. I think we should read poems because...
(a) _____
(b) _____
(c) _____

4. I think is important to talk to others about poems because...

_____

_____

5. My favorite poetry activity (activities) is (are)...

_____

_____

6. Writing a poem is different than writing a story because...

_____

_____

7. The advice I would give a teacher who wants to teach me poetry is...

_____

_____

8. I own at least one poetry anthology ☐ yes ☐ no
If yes, the title is _____

9. A poem is like...

_____

_____

10. Make a choice by circling (a) or (b) for each of the following:
I would rather read (a) a short poem
                    (b) a long poem
I would rather read (a) a funny poem
                    (b) a poem that makes me think hard

I would rather read (a) a poem that's been illustrated
(b) a poem that's not illustrated
I would rather read (a) a poem that rhymes
(b) a poem that doesn't rhyme
I would rather write (a) a poem that rhymes
(b) a poem that doesn't rhyme
I would rather read a poetry anthology by (a) a single poet
(b) many poets
I would rather (a) listen to my teacher read a poem
(b) read a poem by myself
I would rather respond to a poem (a) by talking with others
(b) by writing

. . . .

Celebrating the Work of a Poet

Things

Went to the corner
Walked in the store
Bought me some candy
Ain't got it no more
Ain't got it no more

Went to the beach
Played on the shore
Built me a sandhouse
Ain't got it no more
Ain't got it no more

Went to the kitchen
Lay down on the floor
Made me a poem
Still got it
Still got it

Eloise Greenfield from
Honey, I Love

There are many reasons for selecting the poems that we give children — sounds of words, rhythms, rhymes, their ability to make us think. Gregory Denman (1988) suggests that a poem's function could be represented by a spectrum, with one end being those poems written by "Mr Wordplay" and the opposite end being written by "Ms Serious Poet." And, of course, between

108

Mr Wordplay and Ms Serious Poet, we can offer nursery rhymes, story poems, lyric poems, and memory poems that focus on innumerable topics.

It is important for children to recognize that there are many types of poetry and become aware of purposes a poet may have in sharing his or her thoughts. One way of doing this is to pause and pay attention to the work of single poet, whether it is the rhythmic, humorous pieces of Dennis Lee, the thought-provoking poems of Eve Merriam, or the sharp-visioned, scattered poems of Arnold Adoff.

In our classroom, we often examined the works of a poet during the course of a single week, reading aloud works by poets such as Jack Prelutsky, Michael Rosen, and Jean Little. We went further than merely reading poems by one poet when we undertook a two-week focus study on Eloise Greenfield.

The work of Eloise Greenfield often focuses on black heritage, especially the African-American experience. Greenfield, it seems, writes poetry to help young people think about themselves as they grow up, their relationships, and their citizenship in the world.

I introduced Eloise Greenfield to the class because of the rich material available in a number of her anthologies. Ultimately, I decided to spend time with her word paintings because I hoped the children would join in with her celebration of life, and recognize her depiction of scenes that are, in the words of one of her poems, "always always love."

Greenfield's characters have a sense of dignity, humor, and love. She nurtures her readers as much as she has nurtured characters she writes about. Her poems may be about dreams ("Buddy's Dream"), memories ("Keepsake"), or observations ("Watching the World Go By"). In fact, most of her characters watch the world go by, whether it be a neighbor who has the weight of the world on her shoulders ("Weights"), a girl who runs faster than a leaf flies ("Lessie"), or a congregation singing songs of praise ("In the Church"). A Greenfield poem has a story to tell, whether it's about island people taking a stroll in a sweet breeze ("That Kind of Day"), two friends fighting ("Education"), or a significant historical event ("Harriet Tubman").

For a unit on exploring memoirs, it was the poetry of Eloise Greenfield that best helped the children recognize how writers can examine life events — not only to report chronological details but to explore the significance of those events. For Lucy McCormick Calkins (1991) "memories aren't found, they're composed and invented" (p. 71). When children read a memory poem such as those written by Eloise Greenfield, they are apt to "unpack their childhood." When children are inspired to talk or write about these moments in prose or poetry, they are doing more than reporting timelines, they are exploring the truths that underlie them.

Greenfield, then, provides a strong model for exploring truths and their relationship to life's events. By asking children, "How did this writer do this?" a teacher can invite them to reflect on their own lives. They can enhance their being through reading and writing by finding meaning in moments of their lives.

Eloise Greenfield says it best in her statement that accompanies the collection, *Honey, I Love*: "My deepest aim is to give them words to love, words to grow on."

Poetry Collections by Eloise Greenfield

Honey, I Love: and other love poems
Illustrated by Diane and Leo Dillon
New York: HarperCollins, 1978
In these sixteen poems, a young child celebrates the joys of everyday life: riding a train, skipping rope, going to the store, keeping her mama company, or writing a poem that she keeps for life.

Nathaniel Talking
Illustrated by Jan Spivey Gilchrest
New York: Black Butterfly Children's Books, 1988
Nine-year-old Nathaniel sits on his front porch watching the world go by, thinking about times when he has misbehaved, his friends and neighbors, his daddy singing the blues, and his mama who was always always love.

Under the Sunday Tree
Paintings by Mr. Amos Ferguson
New York: Harper & Row Publishers, 1988
A collection of poems and paintings that evoke life in the Bahamas. Whether it is a group of boys fishing, a policeman directing traffic, or a girl dreaming dreams, the people we meet under the Sunday tree are filled with humor, dignity, and a loving appreciation of the world surrounding them.

Night on Neighborhood Street
Illustrated by Jan Spivey Gilchrist
New York: Dial Books for Young Readers, 1991
A collection of poems exploring the sounds, sights, and emotions enlivening a black neighborhood during the course of one evening. Greenfield offers depictions and insights into childhood and the nurturing world of family, friends, and neighbors.

EVENT 39
· · · · · · · · · · · ·

Exploring the Poems of Eloise Greenfield

The following activities outline an exploration of the poems of Eloise Greenfield that I experienced with my grade five class. I am grateful for the work of Brian Crawford, a colleague and book buddy who shared a similar poetry focus with his students and in turn shared his ideas with me.

Collecting Snippets

Charlotte Zolotow's *Snippets* is a collection of excerpts from her picture-book repertoire. Using Zolotow's book as a model, children can create a collection of Eloise Greenfield snippets, choosing two to four lines of text that appeal to them. Words can be

> Fambly Time:
> When I read this poem
> I felt a funny happy
> feeling inside.
>
> Darrelyn

illustrated with fine black markers and gathered in a class book. (We called our book *Sing a Song of Colors* from the poem, "Song of the Water Lilies".)

Modelling Eloise Greenfield

At the end of *Nathaniel Talking*, Greenfield invites children to write a twelve-bar blues poem similar to "My Daddy" and "Watching the World Go By," written in the style of lyrics called "twelve-bar blues." Each verse is made of three statements or questions. The first two statements are alike, the third is different but still related to the other two and rhymes with them. Each verse is four bars, making a total of twelve bars. Children can try to write a poem based on this structure or they can determine a structure that Greenfield uses to write a poem.

Recognizing Poems by Eloise Greenfield

Poems from the anthology, *Honey, I Love: and other love poems* can be read aloud to the children in one sitting. For this experience, it's best to discuss individual poems only as a follow-up response activity. Children can work in small groups to list the characteristics/qualities of these poems. Children, as a whole class, can participate in a discussion to compile a final list. The list can be displayed on a class bulletin board and revisited after children have read more Eloise Greenfield poems.

How to Recognize a Poem by Eloise Greenfield

— she talks about her family and herself
— she talks about her life in the past
— some rhyming
— she always uses kids
— talks about her growing up
— half story, half poem
— children tell the poem
— writes in first and third person
— poems are strong
— they sound fast
— writes about things she used to do, like jumping rope
— you can picture every word she writes in your mind

112

— "love" is in a lot of her poems
— uses "and" instead of a comma
— uses black people
— mostly girls

Responding to Individual Poems

Each child can be given a copy of a poem by Eloise Greenfield. Children can write a respose to the poem on a small recipe file card, offer a critical comment, write about what the poem reminded them of, or raise questions they had about the poem.

In pairs, children can share their poems with each other. Each pair can compare the two poems, discussing similarities or differences. As an extension, children can work in groups of four, with each student discussing his or her poem. The group of four can then decide on one statement that they feel links all these poems. Children can offer their statements during a whole-class discussion. Poems can be transcribed on a piece of paper and illustrated to create a new anthology of Eloise Greenfield poems. Statements from the children's responses can be displayed on the page facing the poem.

Questions for Eloise Greenfield

As a final activity, children can brainstorm a list of questions they would ask Eloise Greenfield about her work. As they devise their questions, children can reflect on their experiences with her poems and make hunches about her writing process (e.g., *Which of your poems are autobiographical? How is writing a poem different than writing a story for you? Who do you conference with?*)

EVENT 40

. . . .

Fifteen Ways of Celebrating a Single Poet

Some of the activities described on the next pages have been outlined for use in other contexts. Like previous suggestions, those given here can provide a base for exploration for your class. Poets such as Eloise Greenfield offer children a wealth of material with which to work.

1. Choral Speaking
Choose one lengthier poem by the poet and conduct a choral dramatization of the poem by assigning different parts to various members of the class. As a further choral activity, the children can form small groups — each group is responsible for presenting a single poet and must incorporate a variety of speaking parts, loud and soft voices, sound effects, gestures, and formations for the presentations. A choral presentation of the poet's work could be shared with another class in the school or perhaps at a school assembly.

2. Creating a New Anthology
Children can choose favorite poems from various anthologies that feature the poet. Each child could be responsible for transcribing and then illustrating a single poem. A decision should be made about the media that would best serve the poems. Poems could be bound together to create an original anthology celebrating the poet. The class can decide on a title, perhaps selecting a phrase or line from one of the poems.

3. Making a Tape Recording
Working alone, or in small groups, children can rehearse ways to read aloud in order to capture its mood. Each child can contribute to a collective tape recording by reading a poem aloud into a tape recorder.

4. Offering an Opinion
Children can write a review of a poem stating what they like and don't like about the poem, what is special about the poem, and discuss the way the poet presented his or her ideas.

5. Comparing Poems
Children can read four or five poems written by one poet and list points they think connect the poems. What makes the poems similar? What makes them different? As more poems are introduced, children may recognize the style and mood of poems by that poet and identify these points on a list. The class can devise a list *How to Recognize a Poem by* _____.

An alternate activity is to offer the children five or six poems, only one or two of which are written by the focus poet (or conversely, all poems except one or two are written by the poet). Children can discuss which poems they think were written by the poet.

114

6. Borrowing from a Poet

Children might use the title, rhyme scheme, or format of a particular poem to create a poem. They can also write another verse to a poem using the same rhyme scheme.

7. Comparing One Poet to Another

Choose poems by another poet. The style of the tone of the second poet could be quite different from that of the focus poet. Children can draw up a chart, comparing the two poets (theme, length, rhyme, rhythm, vocabulary, mood, feelings, etc.)

8. Dramatizing a Poem

One of the poems could be used as a source for improvisation. If the poem features a character, she or he could be brought to life and interviewed. Children might invent other characters who could tell stories about the character in the poem.

9. Celebrating the Word

Children can design a graffiti wall featuring snippets of lines excerpted from various poems by the poet. They might wish to illustrate the lines they have featured.

10. Going on a Word Hunt

Children can compile a list of new vocabulary they encountered within the poems. The can make guesses about the meaning of the words or discover dictionary definitions. They might compile a glossary by writing definitions of unfamiliar words that they came across. The glossary could used to help others who read poems by this poet.

11. Conducting a Survey

Once the class has decided upon five or six favorite poems by the poet, they can conduct a survey to discover which are favored by younger children, older children, or families. Results can be tabulated on a chart.

12. Examining Titles

Children can offer other suggestions for titles for some of the poems.

13. Holding a Trivia Quiz

Children can work in groups to create a list of questions about a poem or about the poet. Questions can be compiled into a trivia quiz that would test someone's knowledge about the poet and his or her poems.

14. Researching and Further Reading

The class can conduct research and gather as much material about the poet as possible. In some cases, a poet has written other genres. For instance, Eloise Greenfield has written a novel (*Sister*), picture books, (*She Come Bringing Me That Little Baby Girl, Daydreamers*), non-fiction (*Rosa Parks; Paul Robeson*), and an autobiography (*Childtimes*).

15. Contacting the Poet

Some poets are available for school visits. This can help build children's enthusiasm for words as they listen to the poet explain his or her craft. If a visit is not possible, children can write a letter to the poet, describing their reactions to his or her work and perhaps raising questions about poems she or he has written.

Some Questions to Ask About a Poet's Work

- Why do you think the poet wrote these poems? Why didn't they write stories instead?
- What do you imagine the poet looks like? enjoys doing?
- What is unique about the poet's style? How would you recognize a poem by this poet in an anthology?
- What do this poet's poems remind you of? Do you know the people or places described by the poet?
- What things in the poem are there to see? to hear?
- If you were illustrating these poems, what colors would you use? What media would you use for your pictures?
- What musical instrument would best accompany these poems? a drum? a flute? a piano? a violin? other?
- What new words did you learn by reading poems by this poet?
- What changes might you recommend for the poet to make to one or more of his or her poems?
- Referring to a particular poem, where do you think the poet got the idea for his or her writing?
- Are these poems best read aloud or read silently?
- Are any of these poems easy to learn by heart? What makes them memorable?
- How is the reader's imagination used for reading these poems?
- What three words would you use to describe this poet's work?
- If you were to write an introduction to these poems what might you say in two or three sentences?

IX

Poems in Room 203

Give Me Books, Give Me Wings

Give me books,
give me wings,
let me fly
from the page
to a once-upon time
in a long-ago age;
taking off
for an extraterrestrial
place
with brave words
for my flight
through the darkness
of space;
gliding
down
to an ocean's
mysterious
deep
with watery shadows
and pictures to keep;
soaring back
to the earth
and a world
that I know;
give me books,
give me wings
to climb higher and grow.

Myra Cohn Livingston

Collections and Anthologies

Benson, G. (Ed.). *this poem doesn't rhyme*. London, UK: Puffin Books, 1990.

Booth, D. (Ed.). *Voices on the Wind: Poems for All Seasons*. Toronto, ON: Kids Can Press, 1990.

Booth, D. (Ed.) *Til All the Stars Have Fallen*. Toronto, ON: Kids Can Press, 1989.

Carle, E. (Ed.). *Animals Animals*. New York, NY: Philomel Books, 1989.

Cassedy, S., & Suetake, K. *Red Dragonfly on My Shoulder*. New York, NY: HarperCollins, 1992.

Demi. *Demi's Secret Garden*. New York, NY: Henry Holt & Co., 1993.

de Paola, T. (Ed.). *Tomie de Paola's Book of Poems*. New York, NY: Putnam, 1988.

Fisher, R. (Ed.). *Amazing Monsters*. London, UK: Faber & Faber, 1989.

Frank, J. (Ed.). *Snow Toward Evening*. New York, NY: Dial Books, 1990.

Goldstein, B.S. (Ed.). *Inner Chimes: Poems on Poetry*. Honesdale, PA: Boyd's Mill Press, 1992.

Harrison, M., & Stuart-Clark, C. (Eds.) *A Year Full of Poems*. New York, NY: Oxford University Press, 1991.

Hopkins, L. Bennett. (Ed.). *Extra Innings: Baseball Poems*. Orlando, FL: Harcourt Brace & Co., 1993.

Hopkins, L. Bennett. (Ed.). *Still As a Star: A Book of Nighttime Poems*. New York, NY: Little Brown, 1989.

Janeczko, P. (Ed.). *The Place My Words Are Looking For*. New York, NY: Bradbury Press, 1990.

Hudson, W. (Ed.). *Pass It On: African-American Poetry for Children*. New York, NY: Scholastic, 1993.

Kennedy, X.J., & Kennedy, D.M. (Ed.). *Talking Like the Rain: A First Book of Poems*. New York, NY: Little Brown, 1992.

Larrick, N. (Ed.). *The Night of the Whippoorwill*. New York, NY: Philomel Books, 1992.

Manguel, A. (Ed.). *Seasons*. Toronto, ON: Doubleday, 1990.

Moore, L. (Ed.). *Sunflakes*. Boston, MA: Clarion Books, 1992.

Nicholls, J. (Ed.). *What On Earth...?* London, UK: Faber & Faber, 1989.

118

Nye, N. Shihab. (Ed.). *This Same Sky: A collection of poems from around the world*. New York, NY: Four Winds Press, 1992.

Patten, B. *The Puffin Book of Twentieth-Century Verse*. London, UK: Puffin, 1991.

Prelutsky, J. (Ed.). *For Laughing Out Loud: Poems to Tickle Your Funnybone*. New York, NY: Alfred A. Knopf, 1991.

Prelutsky, J. (Ed.). *Poems of A. Nonny Mouse*. New York, NY: Alfred A. Knopf, 1989.

Prelutsky, J. (Ed.). *The Random House Book of Poetry for Children*. New York, NY: Random House, 1983.

Prelutsky, J. (Ed.). *Read-Aloud Rhymes for the Very Young*. New York, NY: Alfred A. Knopf, 1986.

Schenk de Regniers, B., Moore, E., Michaels White, M., & Carr, J. *Sing a Song of Popcorn: Every Child's Books of Poems*. New York, NY: Scholastic, 1988.

Shine, D. Slier. (Ed.). *Make a Joyful Sound: Poems for Children by African-American Poets*. New York, NY: Checkerboard Press, 1991.

Woolger, D. (Ed.). *Who Do You Think You Are?: Poems about people*. Oxford, UK: Oxford University Press, 1990.

Yolen, J. (Ed.). *Weather Report*. Honesdale, PA: Boyd's Mills Press, 1993.

Single Poet Collections

Adoff, A. *In for Winter, Out for Spring*. Orlando, FL: Harcourt Brace Jovanovich, 1991.

Adoff, A. *Chocolate Dreams*. New York, NY: Lothrop, Lee & Shepard, 1989.

Adoff, A. *All the Colors of the Race*. New York, NY: Lothrop, Lee & Shepard, 1982.

Adoff, A. *Eats*. New York, NY: Mulberry Books, 1979.

Ahlberg, A. *I Heard It in the Playground*. London, UK: Viking Kestrel, 1989.

Baylor, B. *Desert Voices*. New York, NY: Aladdin Books, 1993.

Causely, C. *Early in the Morning*. London, UK: Viking Kestrel, 1986.

Dawber, D. *My Underwear's Inside Out*. Kingston, ON: Quarry Press, 1991.

Day, D. *Aska's Birds*. Toronto, ON: Doubleday, 1992.

Day, D. *Aska's Animals*. Toronto, ON: Doubleday, 1991.

Dunn, S. *Primary Rhymerry*. Markham, ON: Pembroke Publishers, 1993.

Dunn, S. *Crackers and Crumbs*. Markham, ON: Pembroke Publishers, 1990.

Dunn, S. *Butterscotch Dreams*. Markham, ON: Pembroke Publishers, 1987.

Edwards, R. *Moon Frog: Animal Poems for Young Children*. Cambridge, MA: Candlewick Press, 1992.

Eliot T.S. *Old Possum's Book of Practical Cats*. London, UK: Faber & Faber, 1939.

Esbensen, B. *Who Shrank My Grandmother's House? Poems of Discovery*. Toronto, ON: Douglas & McIntyre, 1992.

Fleischman, P. *Joyful Noise: Poems for Two Voices*. New York, NY: Harper & Row, 1988.

Fleischman, P. *I Am Phoenix*. New York, NY: Harper & Row, 1985.

Frost, R. *You Come Too*. New York, NY: Henry Holt, 1959.

Graham, C. *Fairy Tales*. New York, NY: Oxford University Press, 1988.

Graham, C. *Small Talk*. New York, NY: Oxford University Press, 1986.

Graham, C. *Jazz Chants*. New York, NY: Oxford University Press, 1978.

Greenfield, E. *Nathaniel Talking*. New York, NY: Black Butterfly Children's Books, 1988.

Greenfield, E. *Under the Sunday Tree*. New York, NY: Harper & Row, 1988.

Greenfield, E. *Honey, I Love: and other poems*. New York, NY: Harper & Row, 1978.

Halloran, P. *I'd Like to Hear a Flower Grow*. Oregon City, OR: Reading Inc., 1989.

Halloran, P. *Red Is my Favorite Color*. Oregon City, OR: Reading Inc., 1988.

Korman, G., & Korman, B. *The D- Poems of Jeremy Bloom: A Collection of Poems About School, Homework, and Life (sort of)*. Toronto, ON: Scholastic, 1992.

Kuskin, K. *Dogs & Dragons: Trees & Dreams*. New York, NY: Harper & Row, 1980.

Lee, D. *Jelly Belly*. Toronto, ON: Macmillan, 1983.

Lewis, J.P. *Two-Legged, Four-Legged, No-Legged Rhymes*. New York, NY: Alfred A. Knopf, 1991.

Little, J. *Hey World, Here I Am!* Toronto, ON: Kids Can Press, 1986.

Livingston, M. Cohn. *I Never Told: and other poems.* New York, NY: Margaret K. McElderry Books, 1992.

Livingston, M. Cohn. *Space Songs.* New York, NY: Holiday House, 1985.

McNaughton, C. *There's A Whole Lot of Weirdos In My Neighborhood.* New York, NY: Scholastic, 1987.

Merriam, E. *The Singing Green.* New York, NY: Morrow Junior Books, 1992.

Merriam, E. *You Be Good & I'll Be Night.* New York, NY: Morrow Junior Books, 1988.

Merriam, E. *Halloween ABC.* New York, NY: Collier Macmillan, 1987.

Milnes, G. *Granny Will Your Dog Bite: and other Mountain Rhymes.* New York, NY: Alfred A. Knopf, 1990.

Moss, J. *The Butterfly Jar.* New York, NY: Bantam Books, 1989.

Nelson, J. *Island Rhymes.* Toronto, ON: Gage, 1992.

O'Callaghan, J. *Taking My Pen for a Walk.* New York, NY: Orchard Books, 1988.

o'huigin, s. *A Dozen Million Spills.* Windsor, ON: Black Moss Press, 1993.

o'huigin, s. *The Ghost Horse of the Mounties.* Windsor, ON: Black Moss Press, 1983.

o'huigin, s. *Scary Poems for Rotten Kids.* Windsor, ON: Black Moss Press, 1982.

Patten, B. *Gargling with Jelly.* London, UK: Viking Kestrel, 1985.

Prelutsky, J. *Something Big Has Been Here.* New York, NY: Greenwillow Books, 1990.

Prelutsky, J. *Under the Blue Umbrella.* New York, NY: Greenwillow Books, 1990.

Prelutsky, J. *Ride a Purple Pelican.* New York, NY: Greenwillow Books, 1987.

Prelutsky, J. *The New Kid on the Block.* New York, NY: Greenwillow Books, 1986.

Reeves, J. *Ragged Robin.* London, UK: Walker Books, 1990.

Rosen, M. *Wouldn't you like to know?* London, UK: Puffin Books, 1987.

Rosen, M. *Quick! Let's Get Out of Here.* London, UK: Andre Deutsch, 1983.

Rylant, C. *Waiting to Waltz.* New York, NY: Bradbury Press, 1984.

Silverstein, S. *A Light in the Attic*. New York, NY: Harper & Row, 1981.

Silverstein, S. *Where the Sidewalk Ends*. New York, NY: Harper & Row, 1974.

Singer, M. *Turtle in July*. New York, NY: Macmillan, 1990.

Wilkins, C. *Old Mrs. Schmatterbung and other friends*. Toronto, ON: McClelland & Stewart, 1989.

Yolen, J. *Bird Watch*. New York, NY: Putnam, 1990.

Yolen, J. *Dinosaur Dances*. New York, NY: Putnam, 1990.

Zolotow, C. *Snippets*. New York, NY: Greenwillow Books, 1993.

Poems as Picture Books

Ahlberg, J., & Ahlerg, A. *Funnybones*. London, UK: Heinemann, 1980.

Baylor, B. *I'm in Charge of Celebrations*. New York, NY: Charles Scribner & Sons, 1986.

Behn, H. *Trees*. New York, NY: Henry Holt, 1992.

Brown, R. *The House that Jack Built*. Toronto: ON: Stoddart, 1991.

Brown R. *A Dark Dark Tale*. New York, NY: Scholastic, 1981.

Dabcovich, L. *The Keys to the Kingdom*. New York, NY: Lothrop, Lee & Shepard, 1982.

Fitch, S. *There Were Monkeys in the Kitchen*. Toronto, ON: Kids Can Press, 1992.

Frasier, D. *On the Day You Were Born*. Orlando, FL: Harcourt Brace Jovanovich, 1991.

Frost, R. *Stopping by Woods on a Snowy Evening*. New York, NY: Dutton Children's Book, 1978.

Kovalski, M. *The Wheels on the Bus*. Toronto, ON: Kids Can Press, 1989.

Kovalski, M. *Jingle Bells*. Toronto, ON: Kids Can Press, 1988.

Martin Jr., B., & Archambault, J. *Chicka Chicka Boom Boom*. New York, NY: Holt Rinehart & Winston, 1989.

Martin J., B., & Archambault, J. *Listen to the Rain*. New York, NY: Holt Rinehart & Winston, 1987.

Marinez, R. *Mrs. McDockerty's Knitting*. Toronto, ON: Douglas & McIntyre, 1990.

Mendoza, G. *The Hunter I Might Have Been*. Los Angeles, CA: Ten Speed Press, 1968.

Poe, E. Allan. *Annabel Lee*. Toronto, ON: Tundra Books, 1987.

Robertson, J. *Sea Witches*. Toronto, ON: Oxford University Press, 1991.

Sandburg, C. *Arithmetic*. Orlando, FL: Harcourt Brace & Co., 1993.

Williams, L. *The Little Old Lady Who Was Not Afraid of Anything*. New York, NY: Crowell, 1986.

Zemach, H. *The Judge*. New York, NY: Farrar Straus & Giroux, 1969.

Zolotow, C. *The Quiet Lady*. New York, NY: Greenwillow Books, 1992.

Nursery Rhymes

Beck, I. *Little Miss Muffett*. New York, NY: Oxford, 1988.

Booth, D. (Ed.). *Doctor Knickerbocker: and other rhymes*. Toronto: ON: Kids Can Press, 1993.

Cole, J. *Anna Banana: 101 Jump Rhymes*. New York, NY: Morrow Junior Books, 1989.

Cole, J., & Calmenson, S. *Miss Mary Mack: and Other Children's Street Rhymes*. New York, NY: Morrow Junior Books, 1990.

de Paola, T. *Tomie de Paola's Book of Mother Goose*. New York, NY: Putnam, 1986.

Foreman, M. *Michael Foreman's Mother Goose*. Orlando, FL: Harcourt Brace Jovanovich, 1991.

Lobel, A. (Ed.). *The Random House Mother Goose*. New York, NY: Random House, 1986.

Marcus, L.S., & Schwartz, A. (Eds.). *Mother Goose's Little Misfortunes*. New York, NY: Bradbury Press, 1990.

Opie, I. *Tail Feathers from Mother Goose*. London, UK: Walker Books, 1988.

Opie, I., & Opie, P. *I Saw Esau: The Schoolchild's Pocket Book*. Cambridge, MA: Candlewick Press, 1992.

Schwartz, A. (Ed.). *And the Green Grass Grew All Around: Folk Poetry from Everyone*. New York, NY: HarperCollins, 1992.

Teacher References

Atwell, N. *Side By Side: Essays on Teaching to Learn*. Portsmouth, NH: Heinemann, 1991.

Barnes, D. *From Communication to Curriculum*. London, UK: Penguin Books, 1976.

Barton, B. *Tell Me Another*. Markham, ON: Pembroke Publishers, 1986.

Benton, M., Teasey, J., Bell, R., & Hurst, K. *Young Reader's Responding to Poems*. London, UK: Routledge, 1988.

Booth, D. *Classroom Voice: Language and Learning in the Classroom*. Toronto, ON: Harcourt Brace & Company, 1993.

Booth, D., & Moore, B. *Poems Please!* Markham, ON: Pembroke Publishers, 1988.

Booth, D., & Thornley-Hall, C. (Eds.). *The Talk Curriculum*. Markham, ON: Pembroke Publishers, 1991.

Calkins, L. McCormick. *Living Between the Lines*. Portsmouth, NH: Heinemann, 1991.

Calkins, L. McCormick. *The Art of Teaching Writing*. Portsmouth, NH: Heinemann, 1986.

Denman, G.A. *When You've Made It on Your Own ...: Teaching Poetry to Young People*. Portsmouth, NH: Heinemann, 1988.

Dias, P. *Making Sense of Poetry: Patterns in the Process*. Ottawa, ON: The Canadian Council of Teachers of English, 1987.

Dias, P., & Hayhoe, M. *Developing Response to Poetry*. Philadelphia, PA: Open University Press, 1988.

Duke, C.R. *Poet's Perspectives*. Portsmouth, NH: Boynton/Cook, Heinemann, 1992.

Graves, D. *Exploring Poetry*. Portsmouth, NH: Heinemann, 1992.

Harwayne, S. *Lasting Impressions: Weaving Literature Into the Writing Workshop*. Portsmouth, NH: Heinemann, 1992.

Hayhoe, M., & Parker, S. *Words Large as Apples: Teaching Poetry 11-18*. Cambridge, MA: Cambridge University Press, 1988.

Heard, G. *For the Good of the Sun and the Earth*. Portsmouth, NH: Heinemann, 1989.

Larrick, N. *Let's Do a Poem: Introducing Poetry to Children*. New York, NY: Delacorte Press, 1991.

Livingston, M. Cohn. *Poem-making: Ways to Begin Writing Poetry*. New York, NY: HarperCollins, 1991.

Livingston, M. Cohn. *Climb Into the Bell Tower: Essays on Poetry*. New York, NY: Harper & Row, 1990.

Maley, A., & Duff, A. *The Inward Ear: Poetry in the language classroom*. Cambridge, MA: Cambridge University Press, 1989.

McClure, A.A. *Sunrise and Songs: Reading and Writing Poetry in the Elementary Classroom*. Portsmouth, NH: Heinemann, 1990.

Mearns, H. *Creative Power: The Education of Youth in the Creative Arts*. New York, NY: Dover Publications, 1958.

124

Moore, B. *Words That Taste Good*. Markham, ON: Pembroke Publishers, 1987.

Parsons, L. *Poetry: Themes and Activities*. Markham, ON: Pembroke Publishers, 1992.

Paul, L. *Growing With Books: Book #3: About Poetry*. Toronto, ON: Ontario Ministry of Education, 1988.

Powell, B.S. *Their Own Special Shape*. Toronto, ON: Collier Macmillan, 1976.

Powell, B.S. *Making Poetry*. Toronto, ON: Collier Macmillan, 1973.

Rosen, M. *Did I Hear You Write?* London: Scholastic, 1989.

Rosenblatt, L.M. *The Reader the Text and the Poem: The Transactional Theory of the Literary Work*. Carbondale, IL: Southern Illinois University Press, 1978.

Rosenblatt, L.M. *Literature as Exploration*. New York, NY: Noble & Noble, 1976.

Swartz, L. *Dramathemes*. Markham, ON: Pembroke Publishers, 1988.

Thomson, J. *Understanding Teenagers' Reading: Reading Processes and the Teaching of Literature*. Melbourne, AUS: Methuen, 1987.

Wells, G. "Talk about Text: Where Literacy is Learned and Taught." In D. Booth & C. Thornley-Hall (Eds.). *The Talk Curriculum* (pp. 46-88). Markham: Pembroke Publishers, 1991.

Wells, G., & Chang-Wells, G.L. *Constructing Knowledge Together: Classrooms as Centres of Inquiry and Literacy*. Portsmouth, NH: Heinemann, 1992.

Index

126

128